LISA CANNING

# THE Possibility MOM

## How to be a Great Mom and Pursue Your Dreams at the Same Time

NEW YORK

LONDON • NASHVILLE • MELBOURNE • VANCOUVER

THE *Possibility* MOM

**How to be a Great Mom and Pursue Your Dreams at the Same Time**



Published in New York, New York, by Morgan James Publishing. Morgan James is a trademark of Morgan James, LLC. www.MorganJamesPublishing.com

ISBN 9781642792645 paperback
ISBN 9781642792652 eBook
Library of Congress Control Number: 2018910677

**Cover Design by:**
Megan Dillon
megan@creativeninjadesigns.com

**Interior Design by:**
Christopher Kirk
www.GFSstudio.com

# Table of Contents

# Introduction

I'll never forget the day I told myself there must be another way. It was a crisp November morning. The sun was shining. Birds were chirping. A thin blanket of snow had just covered my hometown of Toronto, Canada.

I sat in the front seat of my grey minivan, taking in all this beauty—which was in clear juxtaposition to the visual clutter inside my van. When you're a working mom with a bunch of small kids, your van is your rolling office. My purse was bursting with paperwork; tile and fabric samples for my interior design clients bulged out of various bags of all shapes and sizes; a McDonald's bag held the remnants of yesterday's lunch; an interesting mix of goldfish crackers, empty juice boxes, water bottles, and sippy cups littered the floorboard; and multiple car seats of all sizes filled the back of the van—one of which held my seven-day-old daughter, our fourth child in five years.

I had just been released from hospital postpartum and was sore all over. I still had on the bandage where my epidural was inserted, and I was wearing a pad the size of Mount Rushmore in underwear with enough fabric to cover a small city. I was feeling like a sleep-deprived, malnourished, torn-in-all-directions zombie mom.

And I was going into work.

As a small business owner with a demanding interior design business, a regular part of my job at the time was juggling multiple large-scale, top-dollar renovation projects. While I had staff to whom I could delegate, I was a bit of a control freak and refused to let go of many details.

This particular day, I insisted on going to check on a job site where an expensive tile was scheduled to be installed. I knew that if I did not go, it would likely be installed incorrectly, despite having plans and drawings on site. It would be a costly mistake to correct, and I told myself my presence on site really was the best thing for the client. And, I convinced myself, it would only be this *one* time. I would only choose work over my health, husband, baby, kids, and sanity just this once.

That day, I took my brand-new bundle of love into a dusty, messy, noisy, chaotic construction site because I felt like it was the right thing to do. Deep down, I knew it was wrong. My clients, my staff, my husband, my parents, and maybe even my kids also knew it was wrong. No one was forcing me to be there. In fact, the look on the faces of my clients, the trades, and my family confirmed their displeasure with my decision. I was the one who told myself I had no other choice.

That day, I realized my priorities were as chaotic and messy as my minivan. I sat with my head on the steering wheel and asked myself how I had gotten to this place. How could trade workers see I was out of control while I had missed it until this moment? I realized I was off course and out of balance. And that moment was the beginning of the end—the end of jeopardizing happiness and peace for the sake of perfection and control. The end of putting work first and sacrificing the good of my family. I was ready to launch a new phase, a healthier phase, and it was something the old Lisa could never have imagined in her wildest dreams.

## The Twenty-First-Century Mom

Being a mother today is challenging. In no other period of history has there been as many ways for a mother to fail. From whether your child's lunch box is BPA-free, to how long you breastfeed, to whether you work outside of the home, moms experience no shortage of ways to feel like a failure. Sometimes it feels as if you can fail at literally everything, all day. Should you doubt this, please check Instagram or Pinterest to confirm that motherhood has become a competitive sport. Are your cupcakes cute enough? Are your meals organic enough? Did your children begin taking Mandarin or Suzuki violin lessons by age three?

And that kind of comparison is exhausting.

As a mom who runs a business while nurturing our seven kids, I have often felt defeated by the demands of both twenty-first-century motherhood and career. I can't tell you the number of times I have thrown my hands in the air and waved the white flag of surrender.

The image of a juggler, tossing and catching countless balls, captures the mood of modern motherhood. So many moms today are tired, stressed, and pulled in a million directions. They are exhausted from handling endless tasks and responsibilities. When they invest more time at work, they feel guilty for

neglecting their family. And when they invest more time with family, they worry about letting the office down or missing out on career advancement.

And, worse, in addition to feeling like a juggler, some moms also feel trapped, held captive by the demands they place on themselves and the lies they believe about what "having it all" must look like. Life moves so quickly, how can they possibly keep up? More laundry, more meals, more pressure, and more demands are always waiting, which means they are falling short in every direction. Having a moment of pleasure or repose seems impossible.

These moms are trapped in an endless cycle of guilt, pressure, and performance—just as I felt during my "minivan meltdown." And it needs to stop.

Hope is possible. Mothering, following your dreams, and living your best life is possible—all at the same time. You, my friend, can be the Possibility Mom.

Because the reality is we have choices in how we respond to everything in our lives. It might not seem like it all the time, but the truth is we always have a choice—and it's always ours. We choose how to respond when a child is whining. We choose how to respond when our spouse says something irritating or we read a nasty Facebook comment. We can set the number of hours we will devote to work and the number we will give to Netflix.

For the last ten years, I have run my interior design business while raising an increasing number of kids, each born approximately eighteen months apart. Every time a baby arrives, I redesign, reshift, and refigure unique ways to approach self-care, childcare, and work. As a result, I have talked to countless women about "balancing it all."

The most common question I get is, "How do you do it? How is it possible to be a present mother to so many children, a supportive wife to your husband, and a successful businesswoman? How can you do it all?"

Well, get comfortable because I'm about to spill it—all my secrets, opinions, tricks, and tactics—one chapter at a time. These are the secrets I share in my online training courses for moms, and the secrets I share with women I coach one-on-one. But before you lump this book in with all the other parenting books or how-to books or career books, I want to make one thing clear: this book is a possibility book. More than a book about motherhood or work, this is a book about *possibility and hope*. It is me passing along the hard lessons I have learned so that you can have hope in navigating motherhood alongside your passions and career. I want you to know peace is attainable in the chaos that currently surrounds and threatens to engulf you.

If you have ever felt like there must be another way; if you have ever felt the very significant stress of balancing competing demands; if you have ever felt like you just can't do it and feel trapped in the life you live, this book is for you. It is a book of dreaming and scheming and one that will help you uncover the unique possibilities in your life.

## Who This Book Is For

I wrote this book for moms like me: moms who want to live life and live it to the fullest; moms who want to make an impact on their family and community; and moms who desire greatness, who dream big, and who want to do something meaningful with their lives but don't always know exactly how to achieve that.

This book is also for moms who feel stuck and discouraged. It's for moms who want to quit their full-time jobs to be home with their kids, and it's also for moms who might be home full time but want a part-time career outside of the home.

I wrote this book especially for moms who want *more* time—for themselves, for their spouse, for their kids, and for their communities. And I especially wrote it for moms who want to be brave, ask hard questions, and design the life they have always wanted. In this book, you will discover a framework for discovering and living your most authentic, fulfilling life. You *can* design your life around what matters most. And I promise you're going to love it. You can do this.

**You *can* design your life around what matters most.**

## Who This Book Is Not For

Doing this work is not for the faint of heart. Designing your life around what matters most requires figuring out what "most" means to you. And ordering your priorities can take serious thought and deliberate effort. You may have to address difficult circumstances or face realities you have been avoiding. You may have to take bold steps you have been putting off. So if you don't *truly* want to change or engage in the soul-searching work required, then fair warning: this book isn't for you.

On a similar note, this book is not intended to make you feel bad or increase your guilt. Trust me, more than enough ways for us to feel bad about ourselves as mothers already exist, so please know this book is not intended to be another voice of criticism. But I will invite you, challenge you, and encourage you to examine parts of your life that may be out of balance—and that process could get uncomfortable. Please trust that I write in a spirit of collaboration, cheering you on toward something amazing.

## How to Get the Most out of This Book

### Keep an Open Mind

I've read a lot of self-help/life-planning/girl-boss/entrepreneur-strategy books, and often I notice an overlap in the examples, concepts, and stories included. But what I love is that each author offers a different lens through which to view the topic, and each finds a way to insert her distinct voice into the discussion, which can help us learn on new levels and apply the material in different ways. I believe we should never stop learning; potential areas for growth and new perspectives to consider are never ending. You bought this book and cracked it open for a reason, so I invite you to keep an open mind as you consider the concepts I'll present. Even if you feel like you've heard something similar before, hear me out as I introduce my unique take, my hard-earned wisdom, and most of all my heart into this conversation.

### Do Each Exercise

I've created some beautiful downloads for recording your answers to each of the exercises you will encounter as you read. You can access these at www.thepossibilitymom.com/downloads. Or simply grab a notebook, your iPhone, or the back of a school permission form and give some thought to the questions. Again, if you picked up this book, chances are you are looking to grow or change in some way—and I promise the process of change will go more quickly when you actually do the work.

### Favor Progress Over Perfection

Don't worry about having the perfect pen in the perfect color or the perfect cup of coffee in the perfect monogrammed mug to jump into this content. Just start—even if it's for a few moments in the school parking lot at pickup time. I tried to make everything in this book as simple and streamlined as possible. In my life, I don't have time to waste on fluff or filler—and I know you don't either. So trust that every single aspect of this book has been intentionally designed to lead you through a thorough yet efficient process of self-examination. I want you to feel a significant amount of success by the end of this book, but this can only occur when you push pause on perfection in favor of progress.

### Be Brave

Because you were drawn to this book, I am guessing that you have a stirring inside directing you toward change. You know more is possible, and you want to find out how to make that happen. So I encourage you to be brave in the way you answer the reflections and do the exercises. Dare to be vulnerable, check in with your heart, and be honest. As you'll see, being brave is an essential component to finding personal fulfillment and true happiness.

### Believe It Is Possible to Write Your Own Story

In the pages ahead, I am going to outline the framework for how I—and other moms—have been able to raise children, run a successful business, maintain an engaged online platform, invest in marriage, volunteer in the community, and still have a personal life. Regardless of your past, your present, or any current limiting beliefs, you *can* live a full, inspiring, balanced, and exciting life, and you can really, *really* enjoy it.

Is it easy? No. Might it require a ton of trial and error? Yes. Might you fall on your face a few times in the process of trying to figure it out? Absolutely. But is it possible? Is it possible to be a mom, live your dreams, and be happy? One hundred times yes.

**It is possible to be a mom, live your dreams, and be happy.**

So if you're like me and want more time, more freedom, and more clarity, then let's get started.

# 1
# Running on the Hamster Wheel

I never thought I would have seven children. If you had told me in 2007, when Josh and I were newly married, that in eleven years we would have seven children ages nine and under, I would have thought you were nuts.

It's not that I didn't like kids. I have always loved kids. But in my head, having a large family was for someone else, not me. I had *big* dreams. I wanted to work hard; be financially solid; have a life full of adventure, spontaneity, and freedom; and pursue the many dreams I had in my heart. Back then I just could not see how my personal ambitions and lofty goals could work with the demands of a large family.

I was twenty-two years old when I started my television career. Fresh out of university, I was offered the unbelievable opportunity (thanks to a casting-agent mom at my high school who watched me speak at school assemblies) to host a show on HGTV called *Marriage Under Construction*. It was a pretty hilarious undertaking as I had practically no television experience, zero interior design training, and had never designed or renovated a house before. But I was up for the challenge! I never thought in my wildest dreams that the experience would lead me to launch a career and start a business.

After that first show, I sat in meetings with many television executives about the future of my career. There was talk of new programs, national campaigns, and opportunities for product development. I was completely dazzled with the possibility of success, stardom, and fame.

But at the same time, I was also preparing to marry the love of my life, Josh. While shooting *Marriage Under Construction*, I was also planning our wedding. In between takes, I was calling vendors and tearing countless pages out of wedding magazines. So while I was getting ready to launch a television career and my interior design business, I was also getting ready to start my life as a new wife and, someday, a mom. And combining all these roles seemed really daunting to me.

While it was never exactly said this harshly, it was communicated to me by lots of people in the industry that it would be career suicide to start a family so early in my career. In fact, the external pressure was so great that while filming the pilot for a brand-new show, I felt the need to keep my first pregnancy a secret for as long as I could, out of fear that it would ruin my chances for further television opportunities and career advancement.

The worry of what having children will do to a mom's career is a real thing. In 2014, *The New York Times* published the article "The Motherhood Penalty vs. the Fatherhood Bonus,"[1] citing statistics on how children boost your career—but only if you're a man.

---

1 https://mobile.nytimes.com/2014/09/07/upshot/a-child-helps-your-career-if-youre-a-man.html

The opening sentence of the article reads, "One of the worst career moves a woman can make is to have children." That's scary stuff for a woman who has ambition, drive, and a mind set on success.

But here's some fun news: I had one child, and success still came. I had two kids, and success still came. I had a bunch more kids, and success still came. While it certainly isn't easy to attend to both kids and personal goals, it certainly *is* possible.

## But How Is It Possible to Juggle Kids and Career?

Over the years, I have spoken to hundreds of moms at all kinds of events, and after listening to the very real struggles of moms with one, two, or more kids, I have come to this conclusion: *mothers today experience too much pressure.*

The world wide web offers so many ways to fail, so many ways to get confused, so many opportunities to compare yourself to others and feel totally inadequate—all without leaving your house. While I love the internet, it poses challenges other generations of mothers never faced. Never before have the intimate details about the lives of other women—how they eat, how they dress, and how they parent—been so easily accessible with one scroll, one swipe, or one click. A mom can spend hours and hours getting lost in the lives of others while her own life passes her by. As a result, comparison is inevitable. Even the most self-aware of mothers can fall into the trap of comparison when access to the lives of others is so gosh darn easy.

Another stressor for mothers today is an illusion that has developed over the past few decades. Current culture tells us we can, and maybe even should, "do it all." We can look fashionable and fit; crush our goals at work; cook elaborate, organic meals; and make adorable, handmade crafts with the kids. As unrealistic as this myth truly is, mothers jump out of bed each morning on the quest to do it all. But here's the problem: we haven't been given the tools to actually succeed at it.

Sheryl Sandberg has convinced us to "lean in," and we believe women belong in the boardroom. We are determined not to let our gender or any other personal obstacle hold us back from success. I absolutely agree with this attitude. But executing successfully and making these goals a reality is more complicated than most women admit.

So how do you stay on track for a great promotion when you want to be home for a family dinner every night? How do you manage multiple clients and multiple projects when you have multiple kids to take care of? How do you know you're still a "good mom" when you are overseeing so many responsibilities at once? The struggle is real. My hope is that this book will encourage you to think through your current personal demands and also provide practical tools to help you answer the questions you might have about life and purpose.

But first I need to tell you a story about some drapes.

## My First Attempt to "Do It All"

While my husband and I were on our honeymoon in Costa Rica in 2007, HGTV aired a marathon of *Marriage Under Construction.* When we returned, my inbox was full of people asking, "Can you come decorate my house? I love your accessible approach to design. We really, really want you to help us." The ambitious entrepreneur in me said, "Sure! I can do that!" and, voilà, Lisa Canning Interiors was born.

Building your own business is trial and error, and I would say the beginning years were pretty terrible. I didn't make any money. I was really stressed and really challenged. I felt intense pressure to prove myself. But as time went on, I grew into the craft of interior design. I invested in business coaching along the way, and now, ten years later, my business is a profitable one that brings me a ton of joy and creative fulfillment while allowing me to provide financially for my family.

But when our first child came, my business was still brand new. I was taking on whatever work I could get and navigating how to run a business with a newborn. My husband was working at a church, in a position that could barely cover the cost of living in Toronto. So I was determined to figure out how to run a business, make money, bring a child along for the ride, and be a happy mom—all at the same time.

I would say I failed at it pretty epically that first year.

On the outside, I projected happiness and fulfillment. I would bring baby John with me while he was still nursing and cover him with a stylish, patterned nursing cover while I discussed paint samples with clients. I would push him in a beautiful, navy-blue Bugaboo stroller along the aisles of luxury design stores. I wore lipstick and carried beautiful handbags and was always in heels. I definitely looked the part of a young, successful, up-and-coming, hip designer. My baby was like an accessory.

People often told me how easy I made motherhood look. And if I had looked at myself with an outsider's perspective, I would have agreed. But when I was alone, I was a mess. I felt like I was failing at everything. I was anxious, insecure, and generally felt like I was letting everyone down: my clients, my husband, my baby, my friends, and myself. I wanted so badly to prove I could do it all, yet I failed the ones I cared about the most, in the worst of ways.

I remember one challenging situation when John was about four months old. I was working on a downtown condo. Typically, my amazing mother would come with me downtown and take the baby on walks so I could work. She would bring the baby back to me when he needed to nurse. That day, my mom wasn't available and John was particularly fussy after just receiving his four-month vaccination shots. I was feeling the pressure to get this job completed and was guilty about running behind schedule due to some challenges with trades. So even though the baby wasn't feeling well and I wasn't sure how I would do anything without my mom's help, I ventured downtown, fueled by stubborn determination and a need to prove that I could manage it all.

It did not go well.

I was alone in the house, trying to hang drapery by myself, doing on my own what should have been a two-person job. Because of the weight of the fabric, I was having a hard time lifting the drapes and climbing the ladder at the same time. Every time I climbed the ladder, the little rings that attach the curtain to the rod would fall off, and I would have to jump down to grab them again. It was a bit of a comedy routine, as I just kept going up and down and up and down, making no progress. (Side note: I would learn later that when you hang ring-top drapes, you put the rings on the rod *first* and *then* hang the drapes on the rings #facepalm #experienceisagoodteacher.)

All the while, infant John was in his car seat beside me. Our frustration levels were climbing at the same time as I struggled with the drapes and he struggled with not feeling well. His complaint started out as a little whimper, followed by a whine. When it was a cry, I got down from the ladder and tried to nurse him. But that was not comforting him, so then I tried to rock him. But that didn't work. I tried to sing to him, burp him, and nurse him again—nothing. I bounced him up and down until I was in a full-on sweat. Sadly, all those efforts failed.

I now had a red-in-the-face, crying infant and a crumpled mess of drapes in front of me. In that moment, I felt such an overwhelming sense of failure: I could not comfort my child, and I could not hang the drapes. I felt like I was failing as a mom and as a business owner. I could not keep it all together.

And in a moment I chalk up to total sleep deprivation and sheer desperation, I looked my baby in the eyes, and in a way louder voice than was appropriate, I shrieked, "Just tell me what you want and I will do it! I will do anything!!!!"

And then it was my turn to cry.

This was not an isolated event. No, I have hundreds of stories like the drape story from my early years of being a mom. I felt immense pressure to perform and was pulled in so many directions. I was sure I was failing everybody and felt so inadequate. I wasn't sure I could go on. Many times I questioned my existence, exhausted by mom guilt and desperate for a solution to an overstretched life. And it took me five years to realize what I was doing wrong.

## The Hamster-Wheel Period

For the first five years of being a mom, the growth of my business was huge on my list of priorities. After *Marriage Under Construction* aired, along with designing spaces for private clients, I also started working behind the scenes in production design for television shows. The production designer on a show is the person who designs the set, brings it to life, and is responsible for making spaces look amazing for the camera. I've designed spaces for numerous shows on HGTV, including *For Rent*, *The Expandables*, and *Buying and Selling with the Property Brothers* (and, yes, the brothers are as nice as they seem on TV).

Production design is an involved job, with a lot of moving parts. And as I came to learn very quickly, it's not the most forgiving job—meaning the camera waits for no one. Insider secret: while many things in "reality TV" are not real at all, the incredibly short timeline for these renovation shows is. We would pull off in three to six weeks a renovation that would typically take three to six months to accomplish in the real world. And it often took around-the-clock effort to complete the design in that time.

As you can imagine, when I was working in television, I missed a lot of evenings with my family, including bedtime stories and tuck-ins. It certainly required a lot of sacrifice. My kids had less of me for long periods of time, and it increased demands on my husband, who had his plate full with a busy career as well.

Now don't get me wrong. Working in television was probably the best thing to happen to me career-wise as it gave me a ton of experience, with contacts and connections that have gotten me to where I am today. And, to be honest, it may have been manageable if it was the *only* thing I did. But the problem was I was saying yes to everything.

As a hungry young business owner, I said yes to tons of press opportunities, writing opportunities, television projects, and private client projects. While at times I exercised strong time-management strategies, more often than not I would say yes to something, telling myself "I'll figure something out," only to be faced with the conundrum of how the new project would *actually fit* into an already packed schedule. But I was stubborn, and I was determined to make it all work.

Even so, time and energy have their limits. During the busy periods, when I was out there hustling hard as a creative entrepreneur, I would tell my husband to hang on just a bit longer, that this season in our lives was almost over. But time and again, the "season" would expand and stretch until he gave up hope of us having any sane time together. In actuality saying *yes* to everything meant I was saying *no* to lots of things too. And unfortunately I was saying no to the things that mattered most.

Ultimately it did not matter how much money I made or how much prestige, press, or acclaim I received. Being able to reward myself with a new handbag or a trip for my family was temporary relief. It would be temporary relief until I would overextend myself once more and find myself in that same frustrated place of feeling like a failure. There was never a finish line. Heck, I never even reached a rest stop.

And that is why I call the first five years of my parenting life the "hamster-wheel period." I spun my wheels and worked really hard, investing long hours and wearing many hats. And while sometimes I was strategic in the way I spent my time, other times I acted without thinking of the consequences.

And why did I keep making the same mistakes with work/life balance? Because this was my mission those first five years: to prove people wrong and to feel a sense of belonging. And I went about that mission without much self-reflection. While you're running on the hamster wheel, you just keep moving and keep trying, with no time to slow down. I just kept hoping I'd reach the place where I felt complete and whole, like I was *enough*.

## Where Do I Belong?

For those first years of motherhood, I felt like I did not belong anywhere. Some of the faith-filled, stay-at-home moms I associated with did not understand my love for my business and my drive. In not so subtle ways, some even suggested that my place was at home and home was where I should stay.

But at the same time, I did not exactly fit in with the working moms who were climbing the corporate ladder, wearing fashionable clothes, and dining in glamorous places. Just as stay-at-home moms rejected the idea of career, these working moms expressed skepticism toward my openness to more kids and my acceptance of playgroups, spit up, and working through nap time.

**I was measuring my success by the standards of other people, not by my own standards.**

I was getting mixed messages from both motherhood camps, and unconsciously it fueled my desire to prove I was doing something important in both areas of my life. I wanted to prove to the career women that you could have kids and not let your work commitments slide. I wanted to prove that motherhood was attractive and awesome. To the stay-at-home camp, I wanted to prove it was entirely possible to be happy at work and home at the same time.

As a result, I worked excruciatingly hard to build an interior design business that looked successful on the outside, regardless of the personal toll on my family. I dressed to play the part of a successful designer, regardless of whether I could afford the clothes or not. I was constantly looking sideways, to what my colleagues were doing, what my friends were doing, and what the influencers on Instagram were doing. I was never brave enough to look inward at what would make me and my family truly happy. For the first five years of motherhood, I was measuring my success by the standards of other people, not by my own standards.

And you know what? It was exhausting to work so hard to fit the mold of success. The saddest part is that I had very little idea I was doing it. I was so caught up with chasing a dream that wasn't entirely my own that I could not see the forest for the trees. And I had no idea how radically different my life would look or how radically joy-filled my life would be when I stopped measuring success by the standards of others and started designing life on my own terms.

**I believe all mothers can find balance, fulfillment, and extreme joy when they measure success by looking inward—not by looking sideways.**

It was when I stopped caring about others' rules and others' opinions that I realized something truly incredible was locked away inside me, something genuine and authentic and unique to me—and it had been there all along. Only when I tapped into this wholehearted, go-my-own way freedom did I really begin to live.

And the possibilities that are unlocked when we dare to look inward is the theme of this book. Knowing yourself is the foundation to finding balance, fulfillment, and joy as a mom. It is the answer to how I balance seven kids and multiple businesses, and it is the answer for any mom, in any situation, who wants to find balance too. I believe all mothers can find balance, fulfillment, and extreme joy when they measure success by looking inward—not by looking sideways—and bravely design their lives around their own definition of success.

For years and years, I looked outward for affirmation: on social media, in blog comments, and in the opinions of my peers. For years and years, I knew I wanted something different, but I was not courageous enough to ask myself hard questions about why exactly I was not entirely happy. I just kept running on my hamster wheel, repeating the same mistakes over and over again, not making any progress.

Brené Brown is a bestselling author who studies shame and resilience. She has discovered vulnerability and joy are interconnected. Thus, wholehearted, joyful living can only be found after being honest with yourself. She encourages her readers to be brave, to look inside, and to understand their individual life story: "Owning our story can be hard but not nearly as difficult as spending our lives running from it." [2]

---

2 Brené Brown, *The Gifts of Imperfection: Let Go of Who You Think You're Supposed to Be and Embrace Who You Are* (Minnesota: Hazelden, 2010)

Let's stop running from our stories. Let's stop trying to live someone else's life. Let's step off the hamster wheel to live our own story with conviction and purpose.

# 2
# Charting a New Course

An important step on my journey of letting go of what others thought and designing my life around my own standards transpired on a cold November weekend in Colorado Springs in 2014.

Leadership guru, blogger, and podcaster Michael Hyatt was hosting a conference called Platform, aimed at business owners and people building personal platforms. As an eager adopter of his content, I knew I had to be there, so I figured out childcare for my four small kids (at that time, ages five and under), bought my plane ticket, and was on my way to a child-free weekend to focus on my business.

Some of the best leaders in the online business space, including Amy Porterfield, Stu McLaren, Pat Flynn, and Crystal Paine, spoke that weekend. What I expected to learn, I definitely got: tips on how to grow your email list, how to use social media effectively, how to monetize your blog, and the like. But what I did not expect were big fat valuable lessons on what was holding me back from making true progress toward a life I really wanted.

## My "Aha!" Moments

My first lesson was delivered by Crystal Paine, author of the popular blog MoneySavingMom.com. If you have ever met Crystal in person, she really is like sunshine, but she delivered this truth with the power of a thousand rainclouds: "Comparison is the thief of joy."

She would go on to say this quote many times throughout her presentation, and each time it was like an arrow piercing deeper into my heart. Each time she said it, I felt the exhaustion of never feeling good enough wash over me. I also felt release as I let go of the pressure to be something disingenuous and of the unreasonable expectations I placed on myself.

It was as if this moment was the first time I could finally hear and believe that I might just be *enough*. I was open to believing I mattered and that my unique ideas, values, and gifts were important. I even dared to believe that not sharing my gifts would deprive the world of something great.

I'm pretty sure I went through an entire Kleenex box during Crystal's talk. The tissues came out again when Stu McLaren, founder of WishList and Tribe, shared this doozy, a quote from David O. McKay: "No other success can compensate for failure in the home."

Bam. Reality struck me square in the face. I knew, sitting in that brightly lit, mountain-air conference center in sunny Colorado Springs, that if I did not stop living a life defined by the values of others, I was going to fail the people at home, those precious souls I cared about the most.

That weekend I finally said no more and began the journey of designing my life around what matters most to me. And that decision has made all the difference.

I spent five years on a hamster wheel, and it took flying halfway across the United States to bring the spinning to a halt. And while my life is certainly far from perfect and I fall back into old habits all the time, I can confidently say that the changes I made when I got home from Colorado Springs began a journey to greater happiness, more peace, less guilt, and more joy.

## Now It's Your Turn

I pray, through this book, that you might have a similar moment of clarity. Today can be your day to say *no more*. Together we are going to plan how you can live an incredible life. We are going to design a life that matches your remarkable strengths, your particular priorities, and your one-of-a-kind family.

In *The Comparison Trap*, Sandra Stanley writes about the jealousy that bubbles up inside when we spend our time looking at the accomplishments of others, asking, "Why not me?" When we are looking at our online "friends" or putting other mothers on a pedestal, we forget that, as Stanley writes, "God has something else planned for you—something even more perfectly suited to your skills, gifts, and temperament."[3]

Similarly, Brené Brown advises on Twitter: "Morning swims are great reminders for the day: stay in your own lane. Comparison kills creativity and joy." Just breathe, swim the strokes you know, and forget about the woman in the lane beside you. Don't count her strokes or shoot for her timing.

Your plan will look radically different from mine, radically different from your best friends', and radically different from

---

3 Sandra Stanley, *The Comparison Trap: A 28-Day Devotional for Women* (Atlanta: North Point Resources, 2015).

those with whom you've been comparing yourself. But you *can* find the strength and determination to be your own perfectly precious creation. And, bonus, your plan will allow you to live a life with less guilt, less overwhelm, and way more joy.

I want to help you accomplish your goals. I want to help you feel confident, happy, and peaceful. I want you to gain clarity on your story and your contribution to the world. But most of all I want you to feel like you can do it. I want you, as Michael Hyatt says, "To win at work and succeed at life." I believe in my heart of hearts that we are all called to something amazing and that motherhood, professional goals, and personal interests can all work together in harmony for the best life possible.

So let's get started. In the chapters ahead, I want to help you do the following:

1. Identify limiting beliefs holding you back from your best life.
2. Identify your priorities by looking ahead to the future.
3. Identify your why by looking at your past.
4. Identify your most ideal life by dreaming big.
5. Identify boundaries to order your calendar and stay true to your priorities.
6. Identify areas that require courage to get unstuck.
7. Identify and share secret struggles that may be weighing you down.
8. Identify how to make this all stick by learning necessary habits and systems.

So let's get started. Go to www.thepossibilitymom.com/assessment and take my ten-minute test. This assessment charts your current beliefs, priorities, calendar, and approach to life and will give you a sense of where you are currently so that you can have a sense of where you need to go. It's really short, so go do it. Now!

## Let's Get Started

1. Make a regular appointment with yourself to read this book and invest the time to do these exercises. I want this book to do what it was meant to do for you at this exact time in your life. So pull out your calendar and assign a slot to this important work of personal development—just as if you had a meeting with a client or a dental appointment. Prioritize this investment in yourself and make it as important as any other event in your calendar. You might set aside thirty minutes every evening after the kids go to bed or use the twenty minutes of your commute to work or the ten minutes of waiting in the carpool line at your child's school. Commit to go through this book and complete all exercises. Do not let it collect dust on a shelf.
2. Finally, join the community. Come on over to Facebook and feel free to discuss the chapters in the Facebook Group The Possibility Mom Success Circle. Consider it your own reading club with moms all over the world who want you to succeed as much as I do.

Ready to dive in? Let's go.

# 3

# Believing Change Is Possible

I love audiobooks; they are just so convenient for moms who don't have time to sit down and read a book. I listen to audiobooks when I drive, when I am decluttering a room, and when I exercise.

A book I listen to at least twice a year is *The Power of Habit* by Charles Duhigg.[4] Masterfully weaving in stories and case studies to illustrate his points, Duhigg outlines an incredible framework for how to examine and create habits. I listen to it frequently because I find the stories quite inspiring, and Duhigg's framework for examining habits is just so helpful for my life.

One story that really impacts me is the story of John from Alcoholics Anonymous. John, a recovering alcoholic, left the program as he felt like he did not need to go to meetings any longer. But upon the death of his mother, he relapsed and got into a car accident that would have killed his son if, as was typical, he had also been in the car at that time. Realizing he had let things get out of control, John turned to his sponsor for help.

4 Charles Duhigg, *The Power of Habit: Why We Do What We Do in Life and Business* (New York: Random House, 2014).

Although John was an atheist, his sponsor's suggestion to submit to a power greater than himself allowed him to return to meetings and gain control of his alcoholism.

What is interesting to me about AA is that it is not a religious organization. Many people who go through AA are non-believers. An estimated ten million people have gotten sober as a result of AA, many of whom have no faith affiliation. So why mention a higher power in seven of its twelve recovery steps?

As Duhigg explains, AA works—and, more generally, habits can be changed successfully—when one believes that change is possible. Bad habits will always be a temptation, but having faith in your own ability to cope and change is important. Bravely designing a life around what matters most requires searching inner work and a whole lot of guts. It requires a mindset that embraces the notion that change is possible.

For some people, change is hard. When Moses led the people of Israel out of Egyptian captivity, they spent forty years in the desert, and when they were finally on the cusp of the Promised Land, many could not look forward. They kept looking back simply because what was behind them was familiar. Even though what was ahead was far more promising, they grew nostalgic about Egypt—the very place they had been held captive as slaves. Unknowingly, we can become stuck in an unfulfilling position just because it is what we know, just because it's comfortable. "The known" feels safe—even if it makes us unhappy.

I am sure you can see examples of this principle in your daily life: the friend who has a string of broken relationships, all with the same type of bad boy, and wonders why she can't find happiness, or the guy who breaks his diet every month and blames his weight gain on external factors. If we look long enough, we will all see a multitude of areas in which limiting beliefs are impacting our lives.

**Designing a life around what matters most requires searching inner work and a whole lot of guts.**

For the sake of survival, our brains are wired to seek patterns, but what was designed as a protective mechanism can also work against us. If we're told something enough times or do something over and over, our brain will continue to look for that pattern, and that line of thought—that trench, if you will—becomes deeper every time. While this is a good process for healthy habits, it can be detrimental when the reinforced pattern is negative or harmful.

I am no expert in psychology, but I have personally undertaken a vigorous study of my own brain over the years. And what I have learned, as a result of participating in counseling groups, being in therapy for three years, and reading multiple self-help books, is that many of the factors that guide our decisions and impulses are unconscious. Many times we react to certain situations with strong emotions that originate from events in our childhood. Through our past experiences, we unconsciously developed beliefs, and these beliefs now run in the background, influencing our actions. So we often react without even thinking. We simply live out a set of beliefs we never consciously wrote for ourselves.

So, to start designing our lives, we need to decide whether unconscious feelings or beliefs are holding us back. I invite you

to download the "Limiting Beliefs Identification" worksheet from www.thepossibilitymom.com/downloads to get started. Together, we're going to examine some potential "deep trenches" in our brains, ones that might limit us from thinking big and bold and out of the box.

This is an important step to complete *before* we start dreaming. Do not skip this step. Before you can plan your best life, you must identify and challenge limiting beliefs or all your planning will be for naught. Believe me; these beliefs will continue to sneak up, uninvited, until they are faced head-on and defeated.

Using the downloaded sheets, or simply a piece of paper, record the limiting beliefs you now hold. Next I will give examples of how to reframe limiting beliefs to something more accurate and more helpful, but first let's uncover the unspoken beliefs holding you back.

Limiting beliefs are the "shoulds," the "have-tos," and the "musts" in our lives. Even though these beliefs aren't real, they are powerful obstacles that stop us from attaining our goals and living our ideal life.

To home in on your limiting beliefs, pay attention when you say, "There's no way I could do that because . . . ." I often hear this expression in my own head and from the mouths of others. Consider these examples:

- "I want to start a new business, but there's no way I could do that because . . ."
- "I want to have another baby, but there's no way I could do that because . . ."
- "I want to quit my job, but there's no way I could do that because . . ."
- "I want to eat healthy, exercise, and lose weight, but there's no way I could do that because . . ."

Of course, the completion of sentences like these may be influenced by a myriad of factors. There might be very significant reasons why someone should not have another baby or quit her job. But most often the phrase "There's no way I could do that because . . ." simply unearths a variety of foundational beliefs and doubts. If you dig down deep, you might discover that the reasons given reveal the individual's limiting beliefs.

Let's take a real-life example from a conversation I had with a friend of mine who shared with me her longings to have another baby. She was quick to add, "But there's no way I could do that." I leaned in and asked her to tell me more. She went on to share that if they had another child, they would have to move.

As an interior design professional, naturally I was curious. I asked her how many bedrooms her house had. She told me three bedrooms, all currently filled, with herself and her husband and her two small boys. I asked her if she had considered having the boys share a room. She told me she hadn't because both she and her husband had grown up with their own rooms.

I asked her what would need to happen in her house to accommodate another child. She told me she would need bunk beds, a new crib (because she had given her old one away), and other supplies. Eventually, through talking it out, my friend realized her limiting belief. She had a limiting belief around the size of home she had to have to grow her family. Her limiting belief was that every child needed his own room, but when presented with other possibilities that were foreign to her experience, she realized there might be more options than she first considered.

As you can see, the process of reframing a limiting belief can be done by asking a few probing questions:

- Is that really true, or is there another option?
- This might be true right now, but will it be true forever?
- I might feel this way today, but does it reflect reality?

Here's the awesome thing: when you uncover, name, and bring to the surface a limiting belief, it is possible to transform that limiting belief and turn it on its head. This process might take effort. Breaking old patterns often takes many, many, many attempts, but experience has proven it's possible.

And let's talk for a moment about fear. Limiting beliefs can bring to the surface deep fears we are not willing to face, and that experience can make us uncomfortable. But, as Dan Sullivan of Strategic Coach shares, "Courage is never comfortable."[5]

We need a new, courageous approach to our fears if we are going to face and overcome them. Remember, fear simply points

5 https://resources.strategiccoach.com/the-multiplier-mindset-blog/courage-the-key-to-confidence-2

out and clearly identifies an area we need to grow in, and this growth is often the very thing we need to do. In fact, you can't grow if you are crippled by fear and unwilling to confront areas of your life you have been avoiding, stuffing, or numbing.

To get you thinking about limiting beliefs—and their related fears—I composed a list of the most common limiting beliefs I see in today's mom. For each, I include a suggestion on how to reframe it.

## Limiting Belief Number One

**Belief:** Being a mom means I have no free time.
**Reframe:** I have choice in and control over the way I spend my time.

Let's keep it real. When you are a mother, you are often not in complete control of your time. A newborn baby does not sleep on a schedule. A child does not plan when to get the stomach flu. You can't control when a child has a temper tantrum, requires an extra cuddle because he hurt himself, or needs your emotional support and presence because his feelings are hurt.

However, we do have choice in and control over how we spend our time in loads of areas. For example, we have control over how many activities our children are enrolled in after school and on weekends. We choose how we spend our time outside of work and how much time we spend watching videos on YouTube.

Raising children and keeping them alive certainly requires a significant investment of time, but as we'll discuss in a later section, you also have significant choice and control in the ways you spend the remaining hours of the day.

## Limiting Belief Number Two

**Belief:** Being a mom means I have no freedom.
**Reframe:** I design my life around my family's unique seasons.

I remember, when I was a mom for the first time, feeling shackled to my house and my breastfed baby. I felt sure I would never sleep again and missed the days when I didn't have to pack a bag so full of baby survival items that it looked like I was going on a mountain expedition, as opposed to just going to the store for milk.

One of the beautiful bonuses of having seven children is that I have the benefit of experience. I know the hard seasons of life will pass. After all, I have survived the sleepless haze of the newborn stage and come out the other end seven times. I have successfully toilet trained four children. I have navigated countless tantrums and successfully lived through the terrible twos and "threenager" years multiple times in a row.

But when I was going through all these stages for the first time, it felt like I would never, *ever* survive; it felt so overwhelming, so endless. I can remember feeling like a former shell of myself, missing the days when I had more freedom. Certain days and hours seemed bleak; I felt so helpless.

But I can also attest that stages pass. Stages when certain kinds of travel, spontaneity, or nights away, kid-free, might not be possible will pass. Children don't stay in diapers forever. They do grow up and can even become helpful. Remember, the dynamic of a family changes as children go through developmental milestones and parents go through their own seasons, impacted by work, extended family, health situations, and the like. Things change, yet you can design your life around these distinct changes and seasons to great success.

## Limiting Belief Number Three

**Belief:** Children are an impediment to success.
**Reframe:** Success is possible, but it might look different than you imagined.

This is my favorite limiting belief to debunk. The narrative on motherhood I possessed as a young woman, freshly graduated out of university, was far from the narrative I have today. Back then, the story I told myself was that motherhood was the thing you did *after* you had a career. Why? Because a career was more important than starting a family. How on earth could you work on your own success while having children?

**That our success is measured by career advancement and the financial benefits a job brings may be the most common limiting belief surrounding motherhood.**

Go into any Facebook group for moms and you will see what I am talking about. In one group, I recently stumbled upon an honest post from a mom whose maternity leave was coming to an end. She vulnerably admitted that once she factored in daycare costs for her child, the cost of a second vehicle to drive to work, career clothes, and lunches out, her salary would leave them at a break-even point. She didn't really want to go back to work, but she felt the pressure to go back because she thought it would be a waste of her university degree to "just stay home" with her kids. She was also concerned about what the gap in her resume would mean for finding a job in the future.

Within an hour of posting, her post garnered 197 responses, with opinions all over the map. Working moms championed her wanting to use her skills and education in the workplace. Stay-at-home moms defended the position that staying home is a beautiful sacrifice. All kinds of conversations were taking place, some blaming her position on the fact that we live in a patriarchal society, some shaming her for not wanting to stay home, and some simply offering empathy and support. Many who joined the conversation were just as confused as she was. Truly, I can think of no better way to stir ire and passion among a group of mothers than to raise the question of pursuing work versus staying home.

What was most evident to me was how much emphasis some were putting on the importance of career—as if career is the only thing by which a woman can measure success in life. This particular issue—that our success is measured by career advancement and the financial benefits a job brings—may be the most common limiting belief about motherhood and the one that causes the most emotional pain.

We'll dive into this issue more later, but for now I would like to suggest that we reframe success. Instead of defining "success" only by the job title we hold, what if we include other factors, including raising children and creating a safe, secure home environment? Couldn't we all benefit from a broader definition of success?

## Limiting Belief Number Four

**Belief:** Having children means I must put all my dreams and passions on hold until my children are older. It's not responsible to do anything outside of the home while my children are young.
**Reframe:** My dreams and passions don't have to go away because I became a mom. I can still nurture them in appropriate ways.

As Jennifer Fulwiler shares in her book *One Beautiful Dream*, we all have "blue flame" passions that light us up, make us elated, and bring us immense joy.[6] While others might find these interests incredibly taxing, to us they are as easy as breathing. These could be things like baking cakes from scratch, writing a blog, filming YouTube videos, or being active in social causes. Stifling the things that brought us joy before motherhood will make us

6 Jennifer Fulwiler, *One Beautiful Dream: The Rollicking Tale of Family Chaos, Personal Passions, and Saying Yes to Them Both* (Grand Rapids: Zondervan, 2018).

feel like we are dying inside. While we can't pursue these dreams at the sacrifice of our families, these "blue flame" activities must be fueled in even the smallest of ways. It is not irresponsible to pursue the interests that light us up, and we should not feel mom guilt about the time we devote to them.

## Interview with Jennifer Fulwiler, Author and Speaker

1. **What is a mom's "blue flame," and why is it important for a mom to nurture it?**
   "Blue flame" is a term I picked up from a friend of mine. It's a talent you can use to make the world a better place, and it gives you energy when you do it. You know that you've found your blue flame when you feel like you come alive when you do it.
2. **Why do you think so many moms feel guilty for pursuing their passions or tending to their blue flame? Where does this guilt come from?**
   We know that being a mom means serving others, and we mistakenly think that serving others means putting your own interests and talents completely on the shelf. That approach, however, is a recipe for burnout. If you're shoving aside the interests that fill you with joy and energy, you won't be able to keep it up over the long term. I've found that when moms fearlessly ignite their blue flames, they end up with more energy that they can then share with their families.
3. **Finish this sentence: In regards to a mom's gifts and talents and her need to nurture them, I wish every**

**mom knew ____________.**

I wish every mom knew that using your blue flame will look different for you than it will for others—and that it will look different for you in different seasons of life. For one woman, using her blue flame might mean working a forty-hour-a-week job. For another, it might mean carving out time to write a poem once a week. You can absolutely pursue your passions when you're a mom, but you just might have to think outside of the box to find how it will fit into your life.

## Reframe Your Limiting Beliefs

I invite you now to consider (and be honest about) any limiting beliefs you might have by reflecting on the last time you used the sentence: "I could never do that because . . . ." Think about how accurate your response is. If it's not accurate, how could you reframe the response?

Use the "Limiting Beliefs Identification" worksheet from www.thepossibilitymom.com/downloads to get started.

# 4
# Identify Priorities by Looking Forward

I am a big musical theatre nerd. I can sing, from memory, the entire score of several Broadway musical classics, including *Joseph and the Amazing Technicolor Dreamcoat*, *Hamilton*, and *Legally Blonde: The Musical*, which I call a classic.

## *La La Land* and Life Lessons

When *La La Land* came out, I knew I had to see it. The film stars Ryan Gosling (Sebastian) and Emma Stone (Mia) as struggling artists in Los Angeles (LA, as in La La) and follows their pursuit of love and success in the competitive world of LA. The movie is great fun, but it also offers some really important lessons on how the things we say yes to impact the quality and design of our lives.

In the film (spoiler alert), Sebastian's dream is to open his own jazz club. He knows the perfect location and even creepily drinks coffee across the street from it, watching it like a hawk. However, for most of the movie, he doesn't do much to actively work toward the goal. Conversely, Mia hustles hard. She pounds the pavement going to auditions, writes and stars in her own play, and works her butt off (between her shifts as a coffee shop barista) to fulfill her dream of becoming an actress.

One day, Sebastian overhears Mia speaking to her mom on the phone. She is telling her mom that her super-cool, jazz-piano-playing boyfriend is going to open his own club soon. You can hear that her mom isn't buying it, and Mia defends him left, right, and center, ever the supportive girlfriend, though it is unclear if she believes he will actually follow through. Sebastian picks up on this doubt and somehow interprets this to mean that, in Mia's mind, he is better off as a successful, stable, and well-paid group musician, and this assumption sets into motion the slow decline of their relationship.

One poignant scene hit close to home for me. Sebastian, in pursuit of a successful, stable, well-paid position, takes a job as a keyboard player in a cool jazz-funk band headed by John Legend. Sebastian is on tour and never home, so he surprises dear Mia by coming home unannounced and preparing a home-cooked meal in their apartment.

Mia, happy to be reunited with her love, asks when the tour will be over so she can get her boyfriend back. Sebastian replies that it kinda won't be over. As soon as the band gets back from tour, they'll record a new album and then go back on tour again. Mia then presses him, asking what this means for his dream of opening a club. She wants to know how the club fits in with touring and recording all the time, and she also wants to know how she fits into these new plans. Not surprisingly, a fight ensues. The couple parts, with Sebastian feeling dejected that Mia doesn't support this plan and Mia feeling baffled that he is giving up his dream for commercial success.

This scene hit home for me because it so wonderfully illustrates what happens when we don't measure the impact a decision might have on those most important to us. With every yes, with every acceptance of an opportunity, a cost occurs somewhere else in our lives.

In his book *Essentialism*, Greg McKeown poetically illustrates the impact of saying yes to things.[7] He likens life to a closet system: you can't endlessly fill it with clothing without also taking items out. Saying yes to something is actually saying no to something else; the path to productivity and balance is saying yes to the things that are really important and getting rid of the rest.

> **The key is you. *You* have to decide—and declare—what is most important.**

During my hamster-wheel period, I just kept saying yes. Hungry for success, hungry for affirmation from my peers, and hungry for accomplishment, I just kept saying yes—without realizing there was a trade-off, not realizing all the yeses were simultaneously creating a lot of nos. Everything has a trade-off, an equal and opposite inverse. And as McKeown says so poignantly, when you fail to set the priorities in your own life, someone else will.

## Interview with Claire Diaz-Ortiz, Author, Speaker, Productivity Expert

1. **In your book *Design Your Day* you talk about the Do Less Method, a simple way to achieve your goals**

7 Greg McKeown, *Essentialism: The Disciplined Pursuit of Yes* (New York: Penguin Random House, 2014).

**more often, in less time, and with greater peace of mind. What is an example of how this method has helped you in your busy life balancing three small children and a worldwide speaking and writing career?** Basically, saying NO is the hardest and most essential skill we can ever learn, and it's something I struggle with every single day. It's incredibly hard in our crazy busy world to not find constant distraction in the things around us. More importantly, we often actually LOOK for distraction because we have such a hard time making decisions. Sound familiar? The easiest way to actually figure out how to winnow down on the most important things is to learn to say NO more often. The decisions will come.

## Identify Your Unique Priorities

I now invite you to create a declaration of your unique priorities. Then we can design your life so it reflects these hand-picked, true-to-you priorities. With a clear list of what counts, you won't be so easily fooled by every opportunity that comes your way. You won't naively select the good to the detriment of the best.

Let's start with a quick definition of priorities. Priorities give rank and importance to things in our lives and often motivate us to action. If health is a high priority, we will make time in the day to exercise. If spending time with your spouse is a high priority, you will ensure that date night is a recurring habit. If our work is a great priority, we will log long hours at the office.

But as in Greg McKeown's closet example, we cannot make everything a priority. You cannot just keep stuffing your life full of things and expect it all to fit. Even if you vacuum seal the heck out of storage bags stuffed full and pray that everything stays put, eventually the pressure will build to a point and everything will blow up (like that scene with Isla Fisher in *Confessions of a Shopaholic*).

So what is the key here? How do you avoid an overflowing closet and an overstretched life? The key is you. *You* have to decide—and declare—what is most important. Then you must not only let your priorities inform your decision making, but also work hard to keep these ranked priorities top of mind. The next step is to create boundaries to ensure your priorities stay in the correct order of ranking. Periodically do a self-audit: Are you keeping what's important in the forefront? Are you discarding the nonessentials? Are you protecting yourself and your family with clear boundaries?

Here's the thing. Anyone can say family is at the top of their list. Anyone can say health is a priority. But why do so many people struggle with keeping fitness as a resolution, and why do so many mothers lament the lack of work-life balance? Because goals are only as good as the behavior attached to those goals. And behavior takes *motivation* to become habit. So are you ready to get some motivation?

## Write Your Own Obituary

Download the "Write Your Own Obituary" worksheet from www.thepossibilitymom.com/downloads.

I stumbled upon this activity via Michael Hyatt and Daniel Harkavy's book *Living Forward*.[8] Essentially, your challenge is to hit fast-forward to the end of your life, to when your friends and family gather at the time of your passing. Now, imagine

8 Michael Hyatt and Daniel Harkavy, *Living Forward: A Proven Plan to Stop Drifting and Get the Life You Want* (Grand Rapids: Baker Books, 2016).

someone gets up to the microphone to deliver your obituary. What does he say?

At the end of your life, how do you want to be remembered? At the end of your life, when all is said and done, with no more time to hustle and no second chances, what do you hope people say about you? What will your legacy be?

Take a quiet moment, and with an optimistic and dreaming heart, describe the legacy you'd like to leave behind. The idea of this exercise is to write how you want your life to be—even if it doesn't look that way currently.

If you're staring at a blank page and don't know where to begin, just start with this question: At the end of my life, what do I want people to say about how I lived? I've included a bunch of examples over at www.thepossibilitymom.com/downloads to give you some inspiration. And here's mine:

> Lisa Canning was a devoted wife and mother. She was insatiable, creative, and steadfast in her love of Jesus and sharing Him and His holy church with others through her work running Alpha programs and with her membership site U Evangelize.
>
> Lisa was passionate about supporting the spouses of those suffering with mental illness, understanding the unique challenges that come with caring for a spouse with anxiety or depression. Lisa was a pioneer in creating media and removing the stigma around mental illness in marriage.
>
> Lisa was a loving spouse to Josh. She was his best friend. She embraced life with him. She embraced fear with him. And, most of all, she embraced with obedience the path that

God set out for them in all details, including their fertility, their finances, and their vocations.

Lisa was the proud mom of John, Evelyn, Leo, Rose, Joseph, James, and Phoebe. She loved them fiercely, and with compassion she recognized their unique gifts and talents and sought to develop them as individuals within a large family. She made time for play and communicated to her children that success in the home was more important than any success out of the home.

Lisa was a champion of motherhood and fought hard to see this role valued in society. It was her life's work to help mothers realize their importance in society and to realize they could pursue their dreams and be great moms at the same time.

## Questions for Reflection

1. On a scale of one to ten, how closely does your obituary describe your current life? Would people in your life likely describe you in the way you want to be remembered?
2. If your obituary does not describe your current life, what steps can you take to make it so?
3. What is currently getting in the way of your life taking shape in this manner?
4. Edit your lengthy obituary down to three to five main bullet points. Finish this sentence: at the end of my life, I want to be remembered for __________.

   a)______________________________________________

   b)______________________________________________

c)________________________________________________

Lisa's answer:

a) sharing Christ with others
b) putting my marriage and children above all other worldly things
c) championing the value of motherhood

What is one thing you could do today to make your current life more closely resemble the life you want to be remembered for?

# 5
# Identify Your Why

One of the fun benefits of raising seven small children is that I have developed a fairly thick skin. Dealing with whines and demands is basically an occupational hazard when you are a mother—and I get it times seven (times eight if you count taking care of my husband and multiply that number by one thousand when he has a cold), so I've had a little experience in the not-taking-things-too-personally arena.

But this was not the case when I was a young mother. Having children as close in age as we have had them garners special attention at times. We basically take up an entire pew at church. When I cross the street to get to my local park, it's a pretty funny sight as I have children hanging onto my fingers, purse straps, and stroller bar. When I am at the grocery store, it looks like I am quite possibly a trained hostage negotiator. And when I roll up to my kids' school for drop-off and pickup, I drive a ten-seat passenger van that looks like a small bus. All this to say, we often attract a little attention by our sheer size and volume.

I had four children, ages five and under, by the time I was twenty-nine. I feel like your twenties are very much a time of self-discovery and a time when you're still fairly influenced by the opinions of others (at least I was). As a certified people-pleaser, this was absolutely my reality in my twenties. I was very concerned with what people thought of me and quite insecure in a lot of ways.

So when people would either find out I was pregnant (again) or discover that none of my kids were twins, I really let their responses affect me. The most common response to our family size at the time was "Are you crazy?" or "That is crazy" or "Your life must be so crazy." And I would respond with a smile, beaming confidently and offering back some expression about how much I loved my crazy life. But then I would go home to my messy house, with piles of laundry, diapers in three sizes, and crayon drawings on the walls, and I would let the self-doubt creep in: *Was I crazy*? I would start to believe the naysayers. I would stand there and mentally let the opinion of strangers, acquaintances, friends, and family define happiness for me.

While I was happy to be a mom of many kids in my twenties, I wasn't a confident mom. Couple that with being told I was crazy and you can understand that I too compared myself to all the different kinds of moms out there. I would compare myself to moms who worked nine to five in beautiful offices, removed from the drudgery of house chores and constant diaper changes. I even envied my childless friends whose hard-earned money was spent on themselves, on luxury and travel. At times I felt trapped in my minivan and would scroll endlessly on social media, dreaming of a life more put together and more "sane" than my own.

But when I entered my thirties and had my fifth child, something shifted. I simply stopped caring. By the time I had my sixth child, I *really* didn't care. And by the time I had my seventh child, I had come up with enough witty comebacks that people didn't know what to do with me. (I am totally kidding; I am not nearly that quick-witted.) In my thirties something changed, and I wish it hadn't taken me nearly a decade to get there.

## To Become Confident, Clarify Your Why

The first step to remaining solid when confronted with others' opinions and lifestyles is to clarify your why. You must be clear on *why you have chosen the particular path you are on*—especially if it feels like the "road less traveled." Author and strategist Simon Sinek has some really interesting things to say about the power of why. (Google his Ted Talk; it's super worth the watch.) In his book *Start with Why*, he helps businesses and individuals see that your why is a much more compelling story than your what or your how. He states, "People don't buy what you do; they buy why you do it."[9] He argues that companies that can strongly communicate their why will, without fail, outsell companies that lead with their what.

In my thirties, things clicked because as I aged I defined why I was doing what I was doing and cultivated a sense of purpose. All the years of being told I was crazy forced me to answer that question for myself, on my own terms: Why was I doing what I was doing? Why were we open to having so many children? Why was it important to me to work when other moms were staying home?

---

9 Simon Sinek, *Start with Why: How Great Leaders Inspire Everyone to Take Action* (New York: Penguin, 2009).

Figuring out why you do what you do and what motivates you will give you a tremendous mental boost when times are difficult. We are doing this exercise now so that you will be ready the next time you start giving in to comparison and the "if-only" mindset. You must be secure in your decisions, and that starts with being clear on your why.

## Draw Your Life Timeline

A visual will help you see the trajectory of your life. The following exercises are inspired by an activity I found in Simon Sinek's book *Find Your Why*.[10] Gather a few pieces of paper and draw a horizontal line across one. On this line, draw the timeline of your life. From your birth to the present day, record all the key moments in your life, the moments that stick out the most or define you. If you run out of room on one page, grab another and continue your line.

Through this process, you are digging into the past, mining your history, your life story, for the events that shaped the way you look at the world. For example, recall the events that established your trait of perseverance or defined your values or influenced what you now hold dear. Examples of these pivotal moments include the following:

- Key memories of childhood
- College major
- Decision on spouse
- Births of children
- Career highlights and challenges
- Major losses in your life

10 Simon Sinek, *Find Your Why* (New York: Penguin Press, 2017), 59-82.

- Health challenges
- Times when you felt most confident
- Times when you felt most challenged

As you explore events in your history, pay special attention to the times that were painful. Some of you may have repressed these memories as the pain may still linger. However, these trials were crucial to your development—for better or worse. Often pain coincides with change, and how we deal with change is often quite revelatory. Keep in mind, you may learn more of your nature from the hard times than from the easy periods.

I've included a few examples of "Draw Your Life Timelines" over at www.thepossibilitymom.com/downloads to give you some inspiration.

Once you have drawn and labeled your timeline (mine took three pieces of paper), tell the story of your life as it is presented on the timeline. On your computer or phone, film yourself telling this story. Talk as if someone is sitting behind the camera. No one needs to see this, so speak freely and honestly. Your video might be ten minutes, or it might be forty minutes. The finished product depends on your personal story and how much detail you feel like unpacking.

Now watch the video and notice your reactions to the events you described. During which parts are you most happy? Which parts cause you to tear up? Does your body language shift? When are you most animated and most sullen?

You might be thinking, *This is way too much work*, or *I hate seeing myself on camera*. Or you might be thinking, *I hate digging up my past, looking at past hurts; I would so much rather live in the present*. I totally get it, and as I was designing this exercise, I felt all the same things. But by guiding many women through this exercise, I have realized that watching yourself tell your own story identifies key patterns:

- What elements or relationships empowered you to fight through challenges?
- In times of significant struggle, what did you cling to?
- What gave you hope when you felt as if you could not go on?
- During which periods were you truly happy?
- During which periods did you feel most like your true self?

Watching yourself speak and observing when your body language gets animated, when your eyes light up, or when tears emerge can be very helpful in understanding the multidimensional person that you are. Whether we like it or not, we are the sum of our experiences, both good and bad. And sometimes we are not aware how much these experiences have impacted how we function today.

## Interview with Marie-Astrid Dubant, Coaching Client

1. **When you did this exercise as my coaching client, writing out your life timeline made you uncomfortable. Why was it challenging for you?**
   My past is messy and includes significant hurt from people I trusted. I did not want to revisit those experiences and bring those feelings back up to the surface. I'm a positive person who likes to live in the present and really did not want to revisit my past.

2. **What did you learn as a result of this exercise?**
   In doing this exercise, I realized that some of my past experiences still had influence on how I act today, and reviewing them allowed me to examine past hurts I was holding on to and to question why I was allowing them to influence current decisions.
3. **How is your life different today as a result of this exercise?**
   Examining how and why I was hurt in my past, but now with distance from those experiences, allowed me to see how far I have come and how I've grown as a person. It has given me confidence in my abilities, particularly regarding resiliency. While I still struggle with many things in my life, this exercise reminded me that I am capable of great things and that my life does not have to be defined by isolated experiences. I have the power and agency to change my life for the better.

## Now It's Your Turn

Using your timeline, write down any patterns or themes that emerge. These elements will be particular to you, but consider the following insights as examples of what might emerge:

- Strategies that worked consistently to help you overcome challenges
- Words that define your unique personality or outlook on life
- Examples of what you are great at, what people praise you for
- Special characteristics or gifts that make you uniquely you

Additionally, you should also be able to answer these three questions:

1. When am I most happy?
2. If money didn't matter, how would I spend my time each day?
3. What's important to me?

I've included a few examples of "Draw Your Life Timeline" worksheets from other moms over at www.thepossibilitymom.com/downloads. These examples should provide helpful reference points.

Now write the words or themes that kept popping up in your story. Later I'll be referring to these as your "life themes," so keep this list handy:

- ____________________
- ____________________
- ____________________
- ____________________
- ____________________

## Write Your Purpose Statement

Armed with these themes and the self-knowledge you developed through the timeline exercise, it's time to develop a statement that articulates who you are. You will use this statement as a reminder of your purpose. It will restore your focus when times are difficult and essentially help you not to feel crazy when someone suggests you might be.

This is going to be an incredibly powerful statement, as it will strengthen you to combat the pattern of comparison that may be robbing you of joy. Because this statement articulates what is unique to you, it will keep you from living life on anyone else's terms. I wish I had this kind of clarity in my twenties. It would have been so much easier to stand firm while others told me I was crazy for living my life my way.

So how do you build this important statement? Essentially you consider the themes you identified and synthesize those points to come up with a sentence that describes how you operate when you feel (a) most yourself and (b) most empowered to get through a crisis.

One can approach this in many different ways, and while I don't like to limit such a significant statement to a fill-in-the-blank type of response, sometimes it helps to have a little structure. You can totally go rogue regarding format, but here is a great place to start: **I believe ________________________________, and that is why ___________________________.**

For example: "I believe in the goodness of people, and that is why I am generous with my time and talents"; "I believe we are all connected, and that is why I choose to spend my time helping my family and close friends become the best versions of themselves"; or "I believe this life is precious, and that is why I choose to live it daringly and with risk."

I'm going to be honest with you. I have read *a lot* of self-help books and articles online on how to write a purpose statement, mission statement, clarifying statement, etc. Across the board, everyone says this takes a bit of time to accomplish, yet I have rolled my eyes at that statement—every single time. But it is true. Despite my desire to do this efficiently, this is not a quick-fix exercise. It may take some time to develop a statement that is most true, one that best captures your essence. It should clearly identify why you persevere in hard times, why you get out of bed each morning, and why your outlook on life is particular to you.

**I believe God has a plan for my life that is better than my own, and that is why I trust Him with everything.**

Want to know mine? Want to know the real answer to the question "How do you do it?" Here's the answer: I believe God has a plan for my life that is better than my own, and that is why I trust Him with everything.

Now it's your turn. Write your own purpose statement with the help of my "Create Your Purpose Statement" worksheet. My hope for you is that your statement will so resonate with your spirit that it feels good and true when you read it.

# 6
# Your Ideal Life

Let's examine where we are in our journey. So far we have completed the following tasks:

- We've examined and challenged limiting beliefs that may get in the way of true success.
- We've outlined how we want to be remembered and considered whether our current life correlates with those aspirations.
- We've established why we do what we do, especially in times of success and struggle.

Let's now continue dreaming of a life that will reflect the personal growth discoveries we've made. We're going to do this in three steps.

## Step 1: Reflect, Revise, Rejoice

Take all the worksheets you've completed for the last two activities (your timeline, life themes, and purpose statement) and lay them out on a table in front of you. Soak this moment in. This is *you* on paper. How does it feel to look at your past realities and future hopes?

Take a moment and read all the statements out loud. Is there anything you want to revise? Anything you want to emphasize? Anything you want to tweak? You are looking at a succinct overview of your unique personhood. Do you like the person you are looking at?

My goal for these exercises is to help you paint a very clear picture of who you are. You may now be closer to seeing *your authentic self* than perhaps you've ever been before. This is the you that shines the brightest, is most alive, and feels the best. It's the you who feels amazing when fully expressed and the you who feels terrible when asked to conform to someone else's standards. We want to celebrate this fully elucidated picture of you. So take a moment and rejoice.

Of course, you could be wondering *but what if I don't like what I see or don't feel like I have found my authentic self?* If you don't feel the previous exercises have given you a grasp on who you really are, that's okay. This is hard work, and it is a process that may take some time.

As Jon Acuff says, "To be unmistakable is to live out who you are in all your uniqueness and use the gifts you were given. It's the bravery to march into the deep forest of who you are and be that person."[11] Sometimes that forest is scary. Sometimes that forest is full of dense fog, winding paths, yucky mud, and dangerous thorns.

It takes work to uncover our authentic self, and it may even take therapy, reading, writing, thinking, praying, and a whole lot

---

11 https://addicted2success.com/success-advice/17-successful-people-share-how-to-become-unmistakable/

of time before we get comfortable with our findings. But only when we are in that forest—and happy to be right in the middle of it—can we find true freedom and happiness.

So if you feel like you haven't quite found yourself yet, that's okay. Hang in with me on this journey and feel free to tweak and modify your life themes and purpose statement until it feels as if you are staring at yourself in the mirror—and you really like what you see.

Your true self is in you, waiting to be uncovered. You can do this.

## Step 2: Dream Big

Keeping your life themes and purpose statement very much in mind, it's time to dream up your ideal life. You may currently be living close to your ideal, only needing to reconsider a few things. Or your dream life could look radically different from the life you are living right now. Either way, allow yourself to dream big, and do not let the issues of time, money, energy, experience, or location constrain you in any way.

Remember, to leave the legacy we want to leave on the world, we actually have to take action toward those ideals. If we want to be remembered as a good friend, we have to call friends, care for friends, and support friends. If we want to be remembered for the books we wrote or the things we created, we have to actively write or create.

So take some time and dream. Fast-forward the movie of your life to a future version of yourself and record that movie in short sentences. Here are some prompts to get you started:

**Vocation:** What do you do every day that contributes to society or earns money for your family? How much do you work, where, and how often?

**Children:** How often do you spend time with your children? Do you travel? What kinds of activities do you engage in together? What boundaries do you have in your schedule so you are able to spend time with your children?

**Marriage:** What makes your marriage great? How do you keep your marriage healthy? What do you do to spend time with each other, away from the kids?

**Spiritual:** What does your spiritual life look like? What does wholeness and inner peace look like for you? How often do you take time to stop and be thankful?

**Physical:** What do you do to keep your family healthy? How often do you exercise, and what do you do to exercise?

**Friendships:** Who is your support network? Who knows you best, and what do you do to relax together?

**Location:** Do you live in the city, in the country, or by the water? What does your home look like?

Remember you are dreaming of an ideal life that will leave the legacy you long to establish, and it should align with the words you wrote in your purpose statement. This ideal life is *not* about what kind of car you drive or the brand of shoes you wear—although those preferences are fun to dream about too! Rather, this is the life you would be exhilarated to live if you had no limitations.

If this list of prompts is overwhelming or too abstract, a simple way to begin dreaming is to ask yourself these questions: What do I wish I could do more of? What do I wish I could do less of? I've created a worksheet for you called "Your Ideal Life Planner" at www.thepossibilitymom.com/downloads to help you.

The following paragraphs outline my ideal life. I offer my answers to these exercises not for the sake of comparison but for the sake of possibility—the very theme of this book. My life might seem out of reach, unappealing, or unachievable to you, but my life is unique to me. There may be elements that resonate with you, or you may reject most of what you read. Either way, I want to spark your thoughts and further your exploration. Read my answers with your own answers in mind. Be put off or be inspired, but either way, move closer to your vision of the life you want to create.

### Vocation

I am able to help moms live fulfilled and balanced lives. I encourage them to articulate their priorities and singular purpose and then design their lives around these inspiring concepts. I do this through online products, coaching, speaking, and writing. I have a lifestyle brand that creates beautiful spaces and experiences; thus, I leverage my interior design experience. I also work with national brands on sponsorship opportunities on my YouTube channel, blog, and podcast.

I am able to work from any location, due to the digital nature of my business. I employ moms, allowing them to live out their dreams but never at the expense of their families.

I engage in the work of evangelization on a regular basis by running the membership site U Evangelize, as well as consistently running an Alpha program at my local church. I create digital content that reminds Catholics it is their calling to share the good news of Jesus with others. Our team and members are around the globe.

I work no more than four hours a day, with flexibility in my schedule to batch create over two- to three-day periods, taking as much time off as needed and as my life and health require. Work and life are not in constant tension.

### Children

We are always open to more. Whether more means guests, family, future biological children, adopted children, or foster children, if we are called to welcome more for a season or for this lifetime, our love makes room.

I am able to spend one-on-one time with each of my children, fostering his or her personality and particular interests. We enjoy activities outdoors, in the community, and at our church. We value spending time together as a family unit.

Weekends are reserved for leisure and each other. We prioritize people over screens. We are adventurous and try new things as a family. We enjoy discovering the world together and work to ensure we have enough time together. On a regular basis, we eat as a family.

Our children enjoy our empathy and feel known. Secure attachment is a high priority in our parenting relationships. Our children know they are more important than any career accomplishment.

### Marriage

Our marriage is always a high priority. We have regular date nights and routinely make time to be present to each other without our phones. We make time for intimacy as we continue to "date" each other and flirt.

We routinely complete assessments on our family's health in all areas, and we complete ninety-day reviews—as McKeown recommends in his book *Essentialism*—in which we plan our schedules proactively, thus ensuring our family's calendar does not spiral out of control.

We declare our marriage is bigger than any one disagreement. We advocate for mental health and support other couples who also experience the challenge of anxiety and depression in their marriage. We have learned to manage Josh's depression and anxiety. It does not own us or define us. When it is present, we adapt, we respond, and we prevail.

### Spiritual

I go to mass more than once a week and regularly see a spiritual director. I participate in the Catholic sacraments and take a spiritual retreat once a year.

I am courageous in living out my faith daily. I invest in relationships around me and invite others to conversations of faith on a regular basis, as I am always on the lookout for opportunities to share what Christ has given me.

I make a daily examination of conscience. Daily, I am grateful for the breath in my lungs and look to find meaning in suffering.

### Physical

I am a good steward of the health I have been given. Thus, I nourish my body with the appropriate foods that allow me to be strong and healthy and live life fully. I have a healthy bedtime and maintain the habit of rising early. I make rest a priority. I make exercise a priority.

### Friendships

I invest in relationships with friends all over the globe. I am kind to my neighbors and practice radical hospitality. We host people in our home and encourage them to relax and be themselves in our presence.

I enjoy guilt-free the time I spend with friends, and I build friendships with those who accept my authentic self.

### Location

Our primary residence is in a small town in southwest Florida, across from a lake and with a view of the church in the center of town. Our home is full of love, joy, and life. It is furnished with a bit of a beach influence and is light and bright. We make regular trips to the ocean.

We travel between our favorite cities, visiting friends and working with churches in Toronto, Ottawa, Vancouver, Montreal, Halifax, Atlanta, Nashville, Dallas, and more. We love spending time on the water.

## Interview with Rachel Cooper from Rachhloves, YouTube Creator

1. **You have a wildly successful YouTube channel, Rachhloves, that you have grown to over one million subscribers. You also have two small kids at home. What is the secret to your success? How are you able to produce videos on a consistent basis with little kids at home?**

   It's the same "secret" that any parent who successfully juggles a career and a family has: hard work and proritizing! Consistency is king in the digital space, so we've made it a priority to make sure our videos are released on schedule, every week. We find work hours where they're available. With little kids at home, those hours are often when the kids are napping or down for the night. We're blessed to have the flexibility to rearrange our days as needed.

2. **Your husband left his career in law to join you in the business full time. What were the circumstances that prompted this change? What pain point did you have that led you to make this decision? What questions did you ask, or what steps did you take, to come to this decision? How did the decision change your life?**
   The decision at the time was prompted by the birth of our first child, Julia, and the accompanying reality that we couldn't continue with both careers while raising a family. Chris was working eighty-plus-hour weeks trying to build his career, and I couldn't keep up with creating enough content to sustain my channel if he wasn't around during the day. So the choice was to either abandon YouTube or for Chris to put his legal career on hold. We decided that because it would be easier to find another job in law than to rebuild a following online, we would take the risk of putting our efforts toward YouTube.
   The years since then have been very different than what either of us could have imagined when we got married or even at the time we made this decision. We've been able to sustain and grow our business together, and much more

important, we've been blessed with the ability to be home with our family while we work.

3. **It's obvious to me from observing you in real life that you put family first. How do you keep family a priority, with so many things asking for your attention?** I've had to adapt a lot. By nature, I am a very organized and structured person; I crave order and planning, and I am a devotee of Excel. But family doesn't always fit perfectly into schedules and structures. Planning definitely helps, and Chris and I like to sit down and plan out our weeks in advance, but it's always—of necessity—just a big-picture sketch. Which days am I filming? Which videos do we need to have done by what day? When are business calls scheduled? Beyond that, I've had to learn to be more flexible. Sometimes the filming that I had planned to do first thing in the morning doesn't start until after lunch, and that's the sort of thing that used to throw off my whole day. Kids have a way of making you feel more comfortable with chaos, whether you like it or not!

## Step 3: Ensure Priorities Are in the Right Order

Now it's time to make one more declaration of sorts. Completing this step will be very important as we move into the next chapter. We need to order our priorities, and then our actions need to follow that ordering.

Based on your ideal life design, list all the priorities in your life in ranked order. This is the final piece of your unique, authentic life design. Thinking through this piece is vital as we move into scheduling your life and making this all work.

## Putting First Things First

Remember my minivan meltdown? That occurred because my priorities were not in the correct order. In the time leading up to that moment, I had placed my career at the top of the list of priorities, ahead of my marriage, children, health, friendships, and any semblance of personal time. And it did not work. While feeling fulfilled and using our gifts to contribute to society in a unique way is important, it cannot happen at the expense of our families.

**Work should not be our first priority.**

I argue that marriage, children, and health have to be put ahead of career, and this ordering must be reflected in our daily lives. We cannot merely hope this will "just happen"; it has to be a conscious choice. We must *choose* what is given first priority. And work should not be our first priority.

What does this look like? Well, we'll dive deeper into this in the next chapter, but for now understand that putting family ahead of your career doesn't mean giving up on your dreams or giving up what you love. It does, however, mean you have to look at how your time is spent and what that leaves you at the end of the day.

So place the following (and any other priorities you would have in your ideal life) in order of importance, starting with number one: spiritual life, marriage, children, extended family, health, career, friends, and hobbies.

1. ______________________________
2. ______________________________
3. ______________________________
4. ______________________________
5. ______________________________
6. ______________________________
7. ______________________________
8. ______________________________

Phew! You did it! There's a beautiful worksheet called "Managing Your Priorities" you can fill out that will layer all these items together. Download it now at www.thepossibilitymom.com/downloads.

# 7

# Making This Work: The Importance of Your Schedule

My family routinely visits a cottage on Stoney Lake, about two hours northeast of our home in Toronto. It is everything you would want in a Canadian cabin experience: closeness to nature, a wood-burning stove, fresh air, a peaceful lake, majestic evergreen trees, and sunsets so spectacular you need no filter on Instagram. We celebrate birthdays at the cottage, milestones at the cottage, and really treat this idyllic retreat as part of our mental health regime.

During one period of time in my hamster-wheel phase, I promised my family that a trip to the cottage was the reward at the end of a very intense work period. It was what I used to curb the guilt of not being there to tuck them in for bed and sometimes not being there when they woke up.

I would say often to my kids during this period, "Just hang on until we get to the cottage, and Mommy will be all yours." That is an easy story to tell kids, but my husband was sick of hearing that same old song.

## Your Schedule, Your Idols

So when we were at the cottage, I made sure I was available. My phone was off. I felt like we were finally filling up the drained account of quality time spent together. To be really intentional, my husband and I thought it would be fun to do a personal development course I had purchased for us called "5 Days to Your Best Year Ever."[12] The course consisted of videos and worksheets aimed at setting goals for the year ahead.

With two glasses of wine, a roaring fire, and December snow lightly falling outside, we curled up for what I thought was going to be an inspiring, invigorating experience. Instead, the material ripped a Band-Aid off a festering wound in our marriage. As unpleasant as that was, this was another moment that got me to where I am today.

In one of the exercises, you're asked to look back on the previous year, describe it as if it were a movie genre (comedy, tragedy, adventure, romance, etc.), and give it a title. My year was full of accomplishments. I was working in television, creating incredible rooms that would appear on millions of screens around the world on a top-rated show. I was published that year in multiple major decor publications. I was called one of Toronto's top-ten interior designers by a popular blog. I had plenty of money in the bank that was providing worthwhile things for my family. Many professional goals I had set for myself had been accomplished.

With much excitement, I told my husband, "My movie genre is adventure! And my title is *Goals Met*! What's yours?"

---

12 https://bestyearever.me/

And with what I would call an expression of sorrowful sincerity, he turned to me and said, "My genre is horror. And my title is *Vise Grip*."

"What?! What do you mean *Vise Grip*?" I asked him.

"Your work schedule and our lifestyle is excruciating. I feel like I am constantly being squeezed, with no escape."

**"Unhappiness is not knowing what we want and killing ourselves to get it."**

—Don Herold

I chased, for so long, the dream of being an accomplished interior designer. This goal was the most important thing in my life as I held it above all other priorities—including my health—and my actions followed suit.

And even when I accomplished some of my career must-dos (being published, earning a healthy salary, enjoying recognition), the happiness was extremely temporary. It wasn't lasting. It wasn't meaningful. And the pursuit of it came at too great a cost. In short, it was not worth it. I was chasing the wrong thing. Poet and humorist Don Herold wrote a line that sums up this phase of my life: "Unhappiness is not knowing what we want and killing ourselves to get it."

But I didn't see how off course I truly was—or maybe I didn't want to see it—until that night at the cottage. It took my husband telling me he felt like his life was held in a vise grip to snap out of it and make some changes. After the cottage, I took a hard look at my schedule and decided to make some significant alterations. As I mentioned earlier, I was chasing a dream life that wasn't really mine. I had made an idol out of career success and forgotten about success in the home. And to change this, the first place I began was by adjusting my schedule.

## Step 1: Creating Boundaries

Establishing boundaries must be your first step in creating a more workable schedule. You must draw a line between what is most sacred to you and other competing priorities. If you do not clearly demarcate where the essential ends and all else begins, the nonessential will get in the way of or even choke out what is actually most important.

**What kind of boundary can you place around your schedule that will allow you to satisfy your top priorities?**

Prior to Josh's vise grip comment, I was working around the clock. I would work at my computer, work on my phone while taking kids to the park, distractedly check my phone while out with friends, and basically find any moment I could to work—even when in the bathroom on my phone. (Don't judge me. I know some of you do it too!)

In the small crevices of the time remaining, I would fit in family and friends. In the even smaller crevices, I would try to live a somewhat healthy lifestyle. So in the weeks after the vise-grip comment, I decided to try something different. I only took on the kind of work that would allow me to pick up my children from school three times a week.

At first I thought it would not be possible. I thought the sacrifice would be too great. But when I put my plan into action, it worked.

And while I had to say no to some jobs, in general my clients supported my new schedule. And you know what happened? Instead of bending over backwards to meet the schedules of other people, people bent over backwards to fit my schedule. So I have an important question to ask you: What kind of boundary can you place around your schedule that will allow you to satisfy your top priorities?

Here are a few examples of healthy boundaries to help you start:

- Every morning must begin with quiet time. Therefore, I set my alarm one hour before my children wake up.
- I leave the office no later than five o'clock every evening, which means I am tying up loose ends and saying goodbye to people by a quarter of five.
- To conserve my energy, I only go out two evenings a week. Thus, I am able to keep my house in order and give my family the attention they need.
- I travel out of country no more than once a quarter.
- Head on over to www.thepossibilitymom.com/downloads for my "Boundary Planning Guide."

## Who Will You Disappoint?

In her book *Present Over Perfect*, Shauna Niequist describes "concentric circles" as a way to distinguish who to disappoint. This is a helpful visual in drawing boundaries in our schedules:

> Picture your relationships like concentric circles. The inner circle is your spouse, your children, your very best friends. Then the next circle out is your extended family and good friends. Then people you know, but not well, colleagues, and so on, to the outer edge. Aim to disappoint the people at the center as rarely as possible.

> And then learn to be more and more comfortable with disappointing the people who lie at the edges of the circle—people you're not as close to, people who do not and should not require your unflagging dedication.[13]

## Step Two: Increasing Productivity through Deep Work

Most often, the automatic response when I say hi to a mom in the schoolyard and ask how she's doing is "So busy!" And my automatic response is "With what?"

We can fill our time with a lot of things, but are they the right things? Some days I feel exhausted and incredibly busy, but when I look back at my day I realize that I mainly accomplished scrolling through my Instagram feed.

Being busy and being productive are actually quite different pursuits. The world is full of "busy" people; far fewer people are set on being productive. And for a long time I was one of those busy people! I wore the words "busy" and "hustle" like a badge of honor! But, as I have shared previously, it was not sustainable long term.

Instead, consider practicing what author and blog writer Cal Newport calls "deep work," which essentially means you complete a very specific task undistracted for a designated period of time.[14] During this time, you don't check your email, scroll on social media, or organize your linen closet. You don't even pick up the phone if a friend calls.

---

13 Shauna Niequist, *Present Over Perfect: Leaving Behind Frantic for a Simpler, More Soulful Way of Living* (Grand Rapids: Zondervan, 2016).

14 Cal Newport, *Deep Work: Rules for Focused Success in a Distracted World* (New York: Grand Central, 2016).

**What could you accomplish if, on a regular basis, you gave two hours a day to your goals?**

You stay committed to your task for that period of time—whether it be a career-related goal, like writing a blog post or completing a report, or a domestic goal, like cleaning an area of your home or making a costume for your child.

Designating focused time to the things that will move the needle in home or career is a key way to improve productivity and ensure what needs to get done actually gets done. I recommend deep work sessions last no more than two hours. What would you love to do uninterrupted for two hours a day? What could you accomplish in that time? What could you accomplish if, on a regular basis, you gave two hours a day to your goals?

## Step Three: Calendar Audit

Now we are going to do an exercise that is guaranteed to save you some time—or at least get you well on the way to that goal. This activity is inspired by an exercise in the book *Unique Ability* by Dan Sullivan,[15] but our version will be tailored to a busy mom's schedule. This exercise alone, even if you just skimmed and landed on this page, will get you further ahead than where you were before.

Grab several stacks of post-it notes and a marker and a glass of wine. (This might take about thirty minutes, so drink up.) You can also do this exercise electronically using Excel or Google Sheets.

Write down all the activities you currently participate in—literally everything. Make a very comprehensive list of all the activ-

15 Dan Sullivan, *Unique Ability: Creating the Life You Want* (Toronto: Strategic Coach, 2009).

ities you do and/or are responsible for and lay them out in front of you. Be really detailed. Feel free to pull out your physical calendar and examine the various ways you've historically spent your time. Here are some prompts to get you started:

Work

- Emails
- Meetings
- Writing reports
- Marketing
- Accounting
- Phone calls

Home

- Home maintenance
- Grocery shopping
- Appliance repair
- Cleaning
- Decorating

Kids

- Pickup and drop-off
- Driving to activities
- Medical appointments
- Homework
- Bedtime routine
- School appointments
- Playdates
- School committees

- Birthday parties

Personal
- Grooming
- Exercise
- Prayer
- Volunteering
- Time with friends
- Hobbies
- Date night with spouse
- Caring for sick relatives

Car
- Maintenance
- Cleaning
- Gas refills

Now here comes the fun (and feel free to grab my "Conquer Your Calendar" worksheet to help you)! We're going to divide all the activities you have listed into three categories:
1. Things only I can do
2. Things someone else can do
3. Things I should delete

## Things Only I Can Do

This group is very much inspired by what Dan Sullivan would call your "unique abilities": the activities you not only excel in and may be talented at, but you also have a passion for. These things light you up and cause others to say, "Wow! You make that look so easy!" or "Wow! You really look like you are enjoying yourself!"

I also add that certain things, by nature of their role, can only be done by you. For example, *only you can be the mom of your child.* Like no one else, you can nurture, affirm, offer security to, and nourish your child both physically and spiritually.

What are the things in your life that only you can do? It might be tempting to think *only I can do everything on this list*. Yes, it may be the case that you *can* do everything on this list. But should you? Are there things you really need to let go of?

Be ruthless with your evaluation. This is your opportunity to examine, with a new lens, the intentions behind some of your chosen activities to date. Are there activities in your life you are doing because you think you *have* to do them? Look back at your life timeline. Is there anything from your past that motivates something you do currently, but you no longer need to keep at it?

Is there an activity or a committee you are involved in that you accepted simply because there was no one else to run it or you didn't want to disappoint the person who asked you to be involved? Are there things in your life you are doing mainly out of comparison or fear of missing out?

This is where it gets real, ladies. The things we actually, physically put into our schedule are the things that get priority. So be ruthless and brave as you make sure this list is a true reflection of what you stand for and where you want to go.

A quick note on healthy habits: later we will further explore why healthy living is so important to a mom seeking to live her best life, but for now make sure some kind of healthy habit is on this list. Only you can take care of your health.

## Things Someone Else Can Do

This list is comprised of activities that can be delegated to someone else: spouse, babysitter, housekeeper, professional assistant, etc. You might delegate household tasks to professional cleaners or offload elements of your work to an assistant.

Automation can also play a part in lightening your load. We live in an era that offers subscription services: dinners show up at your front door, groceries can be ordered online, and dish detergent and diapers can be delivered on a recurring, automated basis.

Even if you aren't currently in a financial situation to hire out or delegate some of these tasks, go ahead and mark these tasks as activities to hand off eventually. You can always grow into this system, and it never hurts to plan for in the future. Here are a few things that can be delegated or automated to give you more time to do the things that really matter.

Groceries and Meal Prep:

- Some major chains allow you to order your groceries online and then drive to a pickup stall, where your groceries are brought to you. You can bring your kids without the aggravation of saying no to all the treats in the candy aisle.
- Subscription services like Hello Fresh or Blue Apron are amazing options for busy families. A box of food shows up each week with instructions and all ingredients necessary to make restaurant-quality meals.
- For shopping lists organized by aisle and easy-to-follow, detailed instructions to prep five dinners in less than an hour, try http://5dinners1hour.com/.

Cleaning and Home Maintenance:

- Hire a cleaning service. I honestly don't know anyone who regrets spending money on this.
- In Toronto, we have an app called Jiffy where trades people can be hired within hours, meaning vetted pros can fix a leaky faucet, change a light fixture, or clean your gutters fast. No research is required of you, and you will be saved the disappointment of a trade not showing up.

Work:

- Hire a virtual assistant (VA) to triage your inbox, respond to all general inquiries, and fill out forms and paperwork, freeing you up to do what you do best at work.
- Social media can be fun, but it can also be overwhelming. Try automating posts using a tool like CoSchedule or Meet Edgar.
- Go through aspects of your work that are the same process every single time. For example, in my business I used to manually book appointments with clients. When I realized I was doing the same ten steps over and over again—and it was a tedious process anyone could do—I switched to a fully automated calendar booking system called Calendly, which made booking time easier on me and my clients.

## Things You Need to Delete

Free yourself from things getting you no closer to your ideal life. Saying no is hard but necessary if you wish to make room for the things that matter most. This could mean saying no to a book club with acquaintances or deciding not to enroll your daughter in a particular sport just because every other girl in her class is doing it. You might pass on the school bazaar you have organized for the last three years or the afterschool program that causes your family a great deal of stress because of the logistics and timing. Or you might take a break from the nonprofit group you work with, admitting you are only involved because you want to control its outcome.

**Saying no is hard but necessary if you wish to make room for the things that matter most.**

Why can saying no be so hard? We are made up of a sum of experiences, people, and stories that inform how we make decisions—and sometimes this is manifest in unhealthy ways. Sometimes these voices in our head—the ones telling us we aren't good enough, will be criticized, and need to act a certain way—aren't the best voices to listen to. These voices compete with our authentic selves and butt heads with who we truly are. We want to sway one way, but these voices are louder. Even so, we tend to listen anyway and act on the negativity they generate. Why do we do that?

I was raised by incredible parents who nurtured a confidence and resilience in me, for which I am truly grateful. Both my parents exemplified and taught the importance of doing a job well and with integrity. I believe a large part of my success to date is because of their example in this particular area.

But performing well and achieving success can also be very exhausting. It can feel like you always have to be "on" and that being less than perfect is simply not an option. As a result of all the high achievement in my life, the story I told myself was that perfection was necessary for love and acceptance. In my head, acceptance and love were earned by achievement and action. It wasn't enough to just exist—you had to earn your worthiness. And I would go on to project this onto my children, big time.

At first this fixation on achievement was apparent in my approach to their milestones. I would brag with other mom friends about how early my child grew a tooth or how well he adapted to sleep training. I would, with great pride, talk about what an easy baby he was and how he really was just perfect.

But when the first signs of my child falling short of my picture-perfect ideal manifested, I could not deal. I stressed. I Googled. I was a crazy woman in Facebook groups, reading all the comments and giving the opinions of strangers way too much weight.

School presented an entirely new set of challenges, with standards that could be measured and other children and parents to compare against. I noticed I was beginning to doubt some of my parenting decisions when I compared them to the decisions of others. When other parents put their kids into chess club, but my child had not expressed any interest, I would think *should my child do that too*? When my child hit the ice not knowing how to skate, when all the other boys had already been in hockey and skating lessons for years, I thought I was failing him as a parent. Without realizing it, I was making my child into a project and putting emphasis on what he could *do*, rather than who he *was*.

I think Dr. Shefali Tsabary says it best in her book *The Conscious Parent*: "Whether you have an infant or a teen, your children need to feel that just because they exist, they delight you. They need to know they don't have to do anything to earn your undivided attention. They deserve to feel as if just by being born, they have earned the right to be adored."[16]

What does all of this have to do with saying no? Sometimes our agenda is influenced by the expectations of others—some voices we welcome because we respect the source and other voices we don't consciously invite. However, we need only listen to the most important voice when deciding what to commit to with our child: our voice.

Ours is the voice that delights in our child just for being her unique self. It's the voice that doesn't condemn mistakes or errors. This is the voice that may feel like a whisper, drowned out by the opinions of others, but we must learn to listen to our own voice above all else. Our voice must declare that the opinion of others is not going to have power over us.

**It is our spouse, our children, and ourselves that we want to disappoint the least.**

It takes courage—and it's definitely risky—to be authentic. It takes courage to say no to the expectations of others, as we fear we might hurt them or let them down. But the key in being conscious with our schedule is knowing the people we want to disappoint the least. And it is our spouse, our children, and ourselves that we want to disappoint the least.

So be bold and delete everything from your calendar that will not bring you any closer to your ideal life. Say goodbye to all that will move you further away from your family and what

16 Shefali Tsabary, *The Conscious Parent: Transforming Ourselves, Empowering Our Children* (Vancouver: Namaste Publishing, 2010).

you value most. And once you have your new list delineating what you can hand off, what you can eliminate, and what only you can uniquely do, it's time to figure out how to make this work 24-7.

## Step Four: Ideal-Week Planning

Now you need to take your "only I can do" list and actually plot out how you will get all these things done. I hope your to-do list is shorter than when you picked up this book. If so, that reduction is a massive win in itself.

The goal is to schedule all these things out. Literally, go through the list, plot each item into your calendar, and create an automated repeating appointment so it shows up in your calendar on a weekly basis. For example, if only you can write a weekly blog post and you know you need about three hours to write and publish a post, create a three-hour appointment in your calendar from ten to one o'clock on Mondays, for example, and then make it a recurring appointment.

The same process can be followed for child-related activities. If you are the person who primarily picks up your kids from school, put an appointment in your calendar for the amount of time it takes to drive or walk to the school, pick them up, and return home. Repeat this task for all the activities you have on the only-you list.

Once you've entered these activities, you may be thinking, *Okay, Lisa, that's great, but I have now run out of time*. So what happens if you actually block everything in and you run out of hours in the week? If I were sitting across from you in a private coaching session, this is what I would ask:

- Are all the activities in your calendar truly things only you can do? Is there anything that could be delegated to someone else?
- Can any of these activities be batched with something else? For example, could you do research for a blog post on your phone while you run on the treadmill? Can you do phone calls on your commute home or while grocery shopping for your family?
- Is everything in your calendar actually aligned with your ideal life plan? Is there anything on the list that is no longer supporting this plan? Be honest with yourself about things that need to go—even if you are having a hard time letting go.
- Can you reduce the amount of time it takes to do an activity?

This might seem like an incredibly overwhelming exercise, but trust me, it is an incredibly worthwhile exercise. It might seem rigid to schedule everything in your life, but scheduling brings the freedom not to worry about how you are spending your time. You have thought it through, and you know that every worthwhile activity has been accounted for.

This system, my friend, is the cure to mom guilt. When you know you have appropriately scheduled dedicated time for your children, your spouse, yourself, and your work, what do you have to feel guilty about?

## Seasons of Busy

It is important to note that sometimes you will have seasons where your schedule gets thrown out the window. Sometimes work or other commitments overwhelm your calendar for a period because of a time-sensitive need or special project. But the key is to set an end date for these seasons of busy. You cannot live indefinitely in a season of busy.

## Interview with Jackie Lavery, Coaching Client

1. **You balance an at-home, part-time business and life with four small kids. How important is the concept of a schedule in your life?**
   I did not know how important it was until, in my work with you, I did the exercise of examining and creating a schedule. I was very resistant to the notion of scheduling every waking minute of my life. It felt constricting, rigid, and just plain boring. But in living it out, I have seen the freedom that comes from a schedule. I no longer feel guilty when checking emails or spending time on social media because I know I have blocks of time in my day where my phone is away and I am giving undivided attention to my young children. An exercise that I really resisted ended up being the thing that made me feel freer.
2. **Why do you think there is freedom in a schedule?**
   It ensures that I have all the right things in the right places. There is time for my marriage, time for my children, time for my work, and time for housekeeping. Even simple things like grocery shopping, which I used to "fit in" wherever I could squeeze it, now have a spot in my calendar.
3. **What is one way you were able to save time in your calendar so that you could spend time on other things?**

> I run an at-home business that requires me to speak with clients on the phone, and scheduling these calls used to require so much back and forth via email. I have drastically reduced the time it takes to book these calls by using an online service called Calendly that allows my clients to book their call times with me in a streamlined manner, without any back and forth. I now do not worry about missing appointments, and I have drastically reduced my email time, allowing me to free up more time for myself and my family.

## Using Your Strengths to Save Time

The before and after of a remodel on an HGTV show is so much fun to watch. It really is incredible to see a dated, falling-apart kitchen transform—within thirty minutes to an hour—into an open-concept, brightly renovated entertaining space. But the actual process of renovating is much, much harder than the emotional reveal portrays. So much of the effort and angst gets edited out, producing a tidy, linear progression from chaos to order.

In reality, renovation involves hundreds, if not thousands, of steps, decisions, and quality checks to get to the finished product, with many drawings, conversations with trades, and mistakes corrected along the way. Viewers never see the time spent waiting for materials or the unexpected setbacks. Instead, TV shows highlight the renovation magic.

In fact, I wanted my design business to resemble a TV show: room in need of renovation, amazing concept, lighthearted remodeling montage—boom, done. It was the frustrating, in-progress part of the job I was terrible at. I could wow clients in the beginning with understanding their needs and presenting them with a solution that was going to change their lives. I could also wow them at the end with the finished project. But the messy middle of meeting with trades, ensuring quality control of products, and following through with the many, many details of renovation overwhelmed me.

I remember being at a fancy party one evening during my hamster-wheel period—a rare occasion when I was neither pregnant nor had a baby on my hip—with loads of industry peers in the room. My friend Lisa asked me how I was doing, and the tears welled up. I was in the middle of multiple renovation projects and was so exhausted. I had clients who were unhappy with me, and my people-pleasing nature was heavily burdened by their disappointment.

This friend happened to be a fellow designer as well as a trained StrengthsFinder coach. StrengthsFinder is an online assessment tool that helps people discover their natural talents so they can deliberately stay within the bounds of what they do best. My friend promised to send me an email the next day with an explanation of why I found the "messy middle" of a renovation project so hard.

As I waited patiently for this magic email that was going to solve all my problems, I wallowed in self-pity. I told myself I was too young to run my business, that I didn't have enough experience or enough training. I basically told myself I should just quit running my own business and get a job at The Gap.

When the email came, it gave me a feeling of freedom I had not felt in a long time. After reviewing my top-five StrengthsFinder strengths, Lisa told me, in so many words, "you aren't naturally wired for the kind of work that falls in the middle of a design project." I wasn't unworthy or bad at my job. I was struggling because of my temperament and natural strengths. I was dabbling in tasks not in line with my God-given gifts and desires.

The ethos of StrengthsFinder, and other personality tests, is to determine how you perform best based on your natural psychological makeup. Based on my unique strengths, I perform best, as I mentioned earlier, at the very beginning and the very end of an interior design project. The middle, while I can do it, isn't my forte. And what my friend suggested I do, if I wanted to continue project managing renovations of that scale, was to hire staff with those strengths.

But she also said there was another option. Intrigued, I invested in coaching time with her to reverse engineer my interior design business to look completely different from the traditional model. And it's essentially the model I operate today.

My unique strengths are being great at casting vision and developing a plan for people. So my friend helped me reverse engineer my business around my strengths and eventually phase out project managing interior design projects in the traditional way altogether. Now I offer two-hour consultations in which I provide a plan and give people the tools to implement the project on their own.

Now, instead of managing a thousand moving parts, I manage none. Changing my business model has given me the ability to be home for my children after school, and I've basically eradicated a significant source of stress that burdened me on a regular basis. I am able to work fewer hours and have more fun because I am staying within my gifts, rather than trying to improve in an area I was never meant to do.

Maybe you are now thinking, *Well, that's great for you, Lisa, but it could never work for me*. I realize my situation is particular to me and also influenced by the thousands of hours I have invested in the field of interior design. These personal factors have allowed me to transition to this new model, and I don't think I could have done this as successfully at an earlier point in my career.

But even if your business model change isn't as radical as mine or even if you are working for someone else in a job that may not have as much flexibility or fluidity, I can still say with certainty that when you take the StrengthsFinder assessment and implement systems and strategies to stay within your natural strengths, you will be happier and more productive. You will save valuable time you could then spend with people you love, and you will also have fresh eyes to see the possibilities that lie before you. So go ahead and take the assessment at https://www.gallupstrengthscenter.com/ and then take action to order your activities around your unique strengths. I've created a worksheet called "StrengthsFinder Assessment Application" to help you out.

To close out this chapter and finish my thoughts on creating your ideal week, here are some strategies to help you manage your energy and time well.

## Strategies to Manage Energy and Time

### Batching Activities

Consider grouping similar activities together. For example, have certain days of the week where you batch together meetings. On these days, you dress really well, put on makeup, and bring lots of energy. On other days, you could batch more reflective or computer-centered work. You could stay in comfortable clothing and quietly focus on completing a list of tasks. By not ping-ponging between various types of activities, you can increase your focus and save energy and time.

### Limit Your Time

As I mentioned earlier in this chapter, the concept of deep work—limiting how long you will devote to a task—can boost your productivity. Before I had children, writing a blog post could literally take all day. But when you have a breastfeeding baby who is like a human alarm clock, or a toddler who can only sit still long enough for one *Paw Patrol* episode, you learn how to do things in less time. For me, scarcity of time has been my secret to success. Without limits, activities can often expand and take up as much time as we allow. So set limits on your time to increase productivity.

**For me, scarcity of time has been my secret to success.**

### Value Progress over Perfection

Of all the things my children have given me, one of the most surprising is the gift of letting go of perfection. Mind you, this isn't an easy thing to let go of, but experience has shown me that if I stress over every single thing in my life that is not 100 percent perfect, I will end up in the hospital with an ulcer. By their nature, children force us to live outside of ourselves and our selfish desires—and this is a very powerful thing.

I think it's important, as moms, to take an attitude of imperfection toward our schedule. It's no wonder Sheryl Sandberg encourages women to embrace this motto, written prominently on the walls at Facebook: "Done is better than perfect."[17] You might have your optimal week all planned out, but if a child gets sick or an outcome doesn't go exactly as planned, you must learn to adapt. It's okay if it's not perfect. We just have to get started. We cannot become immobilized by the threat of imperfect results or interrupted execution.

It's your turn to get started. So go plan out your ideal week. In the chapters ahead, we'll work on how to make this schedule a habit and discover ways to make the habit stick.

But before that, I want to pause for an honest chat.

---

17 Sheryl Sandberg, *Lean In: Women, Work, and the Will to Lead* (New York: Knopf, 2013).

# 8
# Should a Mom Work?

I think it's important to pause for a moment and have a candid conversation about working motherhood today. A much-debated question is whether a mother's choice to work outside the home will have a massive impact on her quality of life and the quality of life for her family.

As I have shared throughout this book, I have experienced what happens when work overtakes your life at the expense of your family. And I have also experienced the joy and excitement that comes when work and family are aligned and not in tension, when systems are in place that allow a mom to do both.

But getting to a healthy place of alignment is no easy feat. I have battle wounds. And when you easily observe—even in a Facebook group—the divide that can exist between working moms and stay-at-home moms, it's very alarming. This topic elicits heated debate. We need to handle each other with care. My family has done a number of things to balance career and kids. I've seen the merits, and the struggles, of both sides. It's not an easy decision for anyone, and we must extend grace to the mother who lands on the opposite end of the spectrum.

In the early years of my business, we were not in a financial situation to afford any kind of childcare, so during the period when I had a toddler and an infant at home, I juggled my responsibilities; it was a one-woman show. I worked during naptimes and into the wee-hours of the morning while they were sleeping. I enlisted my mom for help with client meetings, and in the evenings my husband held the baby while I sourced products online and created sketches and client presentations. It was difficult. I remember, on more than one occasion, feeling it was impossible to care for a baby and a business.

But my confidence as a mom and a business owner grew with experience. When opportunities arose that I thought would be great, but I did not have the childcare capacity to make it happen, my husband and I would figure out ways to make it work. One such experience was the opportunity to travel to Atlanta to work on the HGTV show *For Rent*. My husband took several weeks of paternity leave from his job, we stayed in a family-friendly townhouse in Atlanta, and he watched the kids while I went off to work.

We had three children when I started working with the Property Brothers as the design coordinator on one of their shows. The job required me to work mainly from an office in downtown Toronto. Since I had run my own business since graduating university, this was my first time joining the ranks of the rest of the working world in the nine-to-five commute.

I remember how free I felt when I first started, how I had the freedom to take a lunch without bringing a diaper bag with me and how I could just sit on a subway and get some reading done without having to find the right Dora episode for my toddler. It was foreign, and it was incredible!

Even more incredible was that my husband, who had been looking to make a bit of a career change, decided to stay home with our three young kids. So for a period of time I was the primary breadwinner while my husband was the primary caregiver. Since then, we have managed children and two careers, with the assistance of my parents and a combination of full- or part-time hired babysitting help.

I share all this to say that I have worn many hats and experienced the pros and cons of working and staying home. So I offer the following opinions and observations in a spirit of love and honest discussion.

## The Benefits of Being a Working Mom

### Fulfillment Through Your Work

When you love what you do, when it is a passion and calling, it can be exciting to work. What an amazing thrill to use your skills, training, and experience in a meaningful way.

This isn't something exclusive to working moms. I believe all moms need to find fulfillment in something outside their duties in the home. Whether it be a hobby, friendships, or pursuing an interest that brought joy before becoming a mom, it's important for every mother—across the board—to explore and grow her God-given passions. I know many women feel really fulfilled in the work they do, and that is an important component of a wholehearted life.

### Financial Win for the Family

Being able to make money for my family is something I thank God for nightly. It is a notion I don't take lightly; being able to provide financially for my family is really exciting to me.

Every family is different, and in some cases it truly is not possible for a family to live on one income, especially if you live in a city with an above-average cost of living. But what I would encourage every mom to reflect upon is how important a particular lifestyle or certain material things are. It's always good to question how one defines "enough."

### Benefit to the World

Some incredible moms use their skills to cure cancer, create policies, shed joy and light and laughter, and contribute to society in meaningful, positive ways. We're not meant to hide our gifts and talents, and I am always on board to support a fellow #momboss.

## Benefits to Being a Stay-at-Home Mom

### Reduced Stress in the Home

It is simply a reality: when both parents are working, stress is added. It can be overwhelming to balance the many responsibilities at work with the many responsibilities at home. This is not to say that being home all day with children is not stressful, but the feeling of being stretched thin increases exponentially when you throw a career into the mix.

And let's be very honest. When two tired parents come home from work, when two tired parents need support after a stressful day, when two tired parents need to navigate who is going to take out the garbage, load the dishwasher, make dinner, or handle yet another up-the-back diaper explosion, it can be a legitimate nightmare.

Does housework get divided fifty-fifty when both parents are working? Do parents take turns taking more of the workload around the house? Does everything get hired out? These questions need to be considered when both parents work.

For life to work, I have observed, a working mom has to either have a lot of support at work, by way of an assistant, a staff team, or really flexible work hours, *or* a lot of support at home, by way of a housekeeper, cleaners, or automated services for food delivery—bonus if you have both. Coming home should not be stressful, and work demands should not bleed over into home life. A sustainable rhythm must be established.

## Work Will Always Be There

This might sound like I am judging moms who choose to go back to work right away, but this is simply an observation. To believe that you absolutely must work because otherwise, in five years, your skills will become irrelevant is a limiting belief. Now, this is of course unique to each individual, but I would say many times, if you were qualified to work in your field before kids, you will likely be qualified to work a similar job, the same job, or some other amazing job when you choose to go back. If you were talented in your job pre-kids, a gap in your resume is not going to matter as much as you may fear—and this fear certainly should not be the driving force behind going back to work.

Children are only young for so long. And there is definitely something to be said for young children having Mom close by. So much of what a child learns about the world is learned at home. Primary caregivers help children develop a healthy sense of self and security, and it's our role, duty, and responsibility to craft that sense of security. If you want to read more, I encourage you to read a bit about attachment theory and the research of psychologists John Bowlby and Mary Ainsworth.

### It Costs Money to Work

The cost of being a part of the workforce is something not every family evaluates carefully. However, in certain situations it costs quite a bit of money to leave the house each day. When you factor in the cost of childcare, lunch out, new clothes and makeup, transportation, and more, it can add up and not necessarily make financial sense for a mom to work. Check out my "Cost of Working" worksheet at www.thepossibilitymom.com/downloads to assess how much it might be costing you to work.

### Societal Pressure

I have had so many conversations with moms who have gone back to work—but didn't want to—and are now miserable. Some felt pressure to go back, as if they would be wasting their degrees and brainpower otherwise. And, yes, while they appreciate the financial benefits that come with work and the advancement in their career, they would rather be home with their children. If outside pressure is the primary motivator for a mom to work, she should consider carefully whose voice she is listening to. The decision to work or stay home is quite personal; make sure you are not inviting friends or extended family members into an intimate discussion meant for you and your spouse alone.

## Interview with Dacia Scali, Coaching Client

1. **Dacia, you're a mom to two kids and have balanced family and career. You recently left a successful fifteen-year career in media with a salary that earned you in the high six figures. What prompted you to leave your job?**

   It wasn't an overnight decision. For about two years, a little voice in my head slowly started getting louder about my lack of desire to do what I did every day. In the media world, you are always on and have to wear many different hats. I realized the hats that were being neglected were my mom hat and my wife hat. I had put my career ahead of my family, as I thought the salary it earned me was how I took care of my family.

   Then one day, shortly after my youngest daughter's fifth birthday, she said the wittiest and on-point reply I'd ever heard. I asked her, "When did you become so clever?" She quickly corrected me that she'd always been that way, but I just never saw her. It crushed me to realize that though I had been around my kids, I was never in the moment with my kids and never truly saw them. Then and there, I knew it was time for a change. They were eight and five, and I felt like yesterday they were babies. I chose not to miss another minute of it. In ten years, they will have their own lives and friends, and I'll have a different role in their lives. I'm fortunate to have a supportive husband, and with a few tweaks, we are making the financials work.

   So I'm going to use these next years to be a mom and

watch what natural talents may present themselves. One day I know I'll work again, but right now I want to work at being a mom.

2. **What has been the hardest part of your transition as you've stopped working outside of the home? What has been the best part?**

   Now, living authentically, the adjustment is harder for those around you. When you finally start living your true life, you show up in ways that are different to how people are used to receiving you—both good and bad. It's been an adjustment, but I've had positive outcomes. I'm *way* more relaxed. I put my kids first, which allows me to feel more connected and present at home.

   I cook again and enjoy providing for my family and friends. I make time for me, which I never did before. Who knew squeezing in a rushed manicure on your lunch break wasn't me time? Self-care was never something I put as a priority, and every mom needs to make it more of a priority. It's not selfish. It's *self-care*, and it's important!

3. **Why do you think so many women feel pressured to work?**

   It's the expectation that the modern mom can do it all. Have *the* job; parent the well-rounded, properly mannered kids; and be the family social convener, all while trying to maintain relationships with spouse, friends, and family. It's nuts that we think we can do all. Honestly, we can and do but at the expense of our self-care. I've removed the phrase "It's okay; I've got it" from my vocabulary because, for me, I choose not to do it *all* but poorly. Instead, I will focus on doing this one thing very well. And you never fail if you choose to be present and make your job as a mother a priority.

4. **What would you say to a mom who wants to leave a successful career but might be afraid to?**
   Jump! The net will always appear and catch you. Because if you think you want this, you likely do, and you will create that net that will carry you through your choices. Life's too short to be in a job you hate.

## Three Factors to Weigh When Deciding to Work or Stay Home

So where do we go from here? In the nine years I've been a working mom, experiencing a variety of approaches for childcare and kids—from my husband being home full time while I worked in an office, to me being home full time while building my business on the side—I've identified three factors a mom should weigh when deciding to work.

### Does Your Job Bring You Fulfillment?

Some women feel immediately fulfilled in motherhood and are able to transition from working to being a mom in a healthy way. They are able to keep other interests alive and feel fulfilled in areas both inside and outside the home. And, in contrast, some women have work that really fulfills them. They have a drive and desire to do their chosen profession. I find entrepreneurs are a special breed; for them, work is fun, satisfying, and stimulating.

I know many women who have had incredibly fulfilling careers, and then, when they stay home to raise children, they aren't quite sure what to do with themselves. They question their identity, feel like they aren't accomplishing anything, and question if they matter outside their regular routine of diapers and laundry.

It can be a very difficult transition to go from being so heavily defined by career to this new role of motherhood. And this is why it is so important for *all* moms to remain interested and invested in the passions they had before having children. This could mean you continue to read professional publications in your field, attend networking or industry events when you are able, or stay on the pulse of your given interest through social media.

In this conversation, I want to also note that motherhood is a full-time job. No one but you can be the mother of your child. No one else can breastfeed or pump milk. You are irreplaceable and important. Your job as your child's mother matters.

It is an accomplishment to keep a child fed, dressed, bathed, nurtured, and loved every single day. Keeping your child alive is a victory! And while it can feel so difficult, especially in the beginning when you are exhausted and feeling like a shell of your former self, I would encourage you to change your mindset. You are a mother. And even though it can feel like you aren't "doing" anything by being home all day with a baby, you are accomplishing the work of being that child's hero, *every single day*.

### Is Working a Strategic Financial Win?

Each family is unique when it comes to financial wisdom and planning, but a few general truths come to mind immediately. Money can be such a powerful tool for change. But one thing

I have observed is that some parents believe that children are expensive and so they work their tails off to provide a good life for their children.

This is just my humble opinion, but the notion that children are expensive is false. As I see it, they are only as expensive as we allow them to be. In the same way I encouraged you to rank your priorities in an earlier exercise, you must also rank the needs of your children. While certain essentials are non-negotiable, other "needs" are nice to have but unnecessary. Defining what is "necessary" or "enough" is a distinction each family must make for itself. In our house, while not always easy, love makes room, and somehow we always have enough.

### Will Working Bring a Significant Amount of Stress into the Home?

I recently watched a collaboration[18] between some of my favorite YouTube mom personalities. Each of the moms took on a decade, pretending to live life as a mom in the 1950s, 1960s, 1970s, 1980s, and 1990s. These women were committed, staying true to the time period in dress, makeup, food, entertainment, and how they interacted with their children and husband.

The stark contrast between the 1950s and 1960s moms and those of the 1980s and 1990s was fascinating. In the '50s and '60s,

---

18 DAY IN THE LIFE OF A 1950s HOUSEWIFE (Brittany Bits of Paradis): https://youtu.be/ShsdZAGhYaQ
DAY IN THE LIFE OF A 1960s HOUSEWIFE (Emily Norris): https://youtu.be/Ync2NTUbXL0
DAY IN THE LIFE OF A 1970s HOUSEWIFE (Elle Lindquist): https://www.youtube.com/watch?v=JE8hLBVAfNk&t=3s
DAY IN THE LIFE OF A 1980s HOUSEWIFE (Shaylee and Baby): https://youtu.be/6dmoXlWzfI4
DAY IN THE LIFE OF A 1990s HOUSEWIFE (Arianna Pflederer): https://youtu.be/OjV2R3MyedY

women were home and therefore emphasis was placed on how she took care of her home and family. When her husband came home from work, there was a beautiful meal prepared. She was attentive to her own appearance, freshening up her makeup and perfume before her husband walked in the house. She served her husband a drink, and the house was relatively peaceful for the evening. Conversely, the 1980s and 1990s moms worked all day, came home to a messy house, and prepared a processed TV dinner in the microwave.

While I won't get into a debate over a woman's place in society in the '50s and '60s, I do think this fun YouTube collaboration showcased the impact of two working parents on the general peace in the home. I also came across a blog post by Jami Ingledue that addresses this same issue.[19] In this blog post, she describes how it is most typically the woman who carries a long mental list that keeps her home and family organized, and this list can be an exhausting thing to carry. The "mental load" that burdens many women—sometimes called "invisible work"—is amplified to a whole other level when a mom works.

## One Final Note

In 2016, James Clear wrote an article[20] about "The Four Burners Theory." This theory, related in *The New Yorker* by David Sedaris, posits the following: imagine your life is represented by a stove with four burners. Each burner symbolizes one major quadrant of your life. The first burner represents your family. The second burner is your friends. The third burner is your health. The fourth burner is your work. The Four Burners Theory says that "to be successful you

19 https://thewildword.com/invisible-work-motherhood/
20 https://jamesclear.com/four-burners-theory

have to cut off one of your burners. And to be really successful you have to cut off two." This theory illustrates the simple fact that it is difficult to do it all, at the same capacity, and do it all well.

All I share is personal observation. I write in hopes of generating thought or discussion with your spouse. While I can't speak directly into your experience, I can offer that, in speaking with other mothers, I hear how many moms feel pressured—either to work or to stay home. The three factors listed in this chapter are a great place to begin questioning what you really want. If you are reading this and realize you do want to make a change, I invite you to go back to your ideal life design and change it until you are satisfied.

A woman's role in society has grown and evolved in wonderful ways in our modern era, but let's not mistake change for a solution.

## Interview with Anna Runyan of ClassyCareerGirl.com

1. **Anna, you are now the founder and CEO of ClassyCareerGirl.com, but you previously worked for a top consulting company in the United States for eight years. You climbed the corporate ladder. You traveled all around the country. You achieved financial success and impact. But you felt unhappy, confused, and stuck. What was the change you were desiring?**
   I was desiring a way to use my strengths more, to have more of an impact and do more of what I loved. I was in finance and realized I didn't like finance, but I loved teaching, mentoring, and coaching about anything, including finance. Once I found out the type of work I enjoyed doing, I tried to do more training and mentoring

in my current role.

Ultimately, though, I had a lot of ideas and goals, and it was hard to implement these in the corporate environment. There was always a boss I had to check with or a client I had to get approval from to make things happen. I didn't want to have to wait to see my ideas happen. Also, a big reason for my change was that I was struggling with infertility and had two miscarriages over two years while at my corporate job. I knew that when my future child arrived, I didn't want to be stressed and overwhelmed anymore or have clients call me on nights and weekends. So I started designing my dream future life while I was still in my corporate job.

2. **What did you have to do to make this change? Was it a scary decision?**

   I first asked to go part time, which was only possible because my husband and I had gotten out of debt years ago. My scary decision was to stop trying to get promoted and be the CEO in the corporate world someday but instead put my time and energy into growing my own business. My scary decision was also taking a pay cut and having everyone (including my parents) think I was completely crazy to walk away from a "secure" job.

   The week after my second miscarriage, I created a presentation for my client and my boss about how it would benefit the team if I went part time. I positioned it so that it was actually a positive for them and me. They accepted the proposal, and I worked part time from home for two years. That's when I got pregnant with my miracle baby and had an incredible pregnancy after cutting the stress out of my life and pursuing my blog as a business because it was something that made me so happy. That's why I am such a big proponent of going toward your dreams and goals and being fulfilled in your professional life because so much can happen in your personal life when you are happy professionally too.

3. **What have been the benefits of leaving your corporate job and working from home on your online membership communities? What are the pros and cons of working from home?**
   Setting your own schedule is a huge benefit. I can walk my daughter to school or take her to the park whenever I need to. I can work in the mornings or nights and spend the days with my daughter. When my daughter was a baby, I did a lot of work during nap time, and I was able to be with her as much as possible. I also like that I can go to the gym when I want and make time for seeing my family. My schedule is basically focused on my family first.
   One of the negatives, though, is that I've had to realize I am not Superwoman. When my daughter was born, I thought I could do it all. I thought I could go grocery shopping, feed and take care of the baby, cook, clean, and grow my business. I didn't even have a schedule for myself, and I was overwhelmed. I realized that I needed to ask for more help, and I had a long conversation with my husband about it. That's when he decided to quit his job as well to help raise our daughter and take on the operations and advertising side of our business.

4. **Your husband quit his job as a budget and operations analyst at a university so he could work in your company. What is it like to work with your spouse?**
   It's not as easy as you might think. In the beginning, it was tough. Everything was in my head, and I had never written down one system or process in my business. Oops! So John had to step in and try to figure things out himself. I also didn't really understand what his strengths or my strengths were so what we thought he would be doing in the beginning, four years ago, is absolutely nothing like what he is doing today.
   Luckily, we were flexible, and when we finally saw what he got really excited about (automating and improving processes), he started taking on more of the stuff he really enjoyed. Our business grew when we both got more aligned with our strengths and found mentors who could teach us more than we knew ourselves. Today we have limited time to work together, so we really try to make it count. We do a lot of work at night and also put vacations and date nights on our calendar so that we can give ourselves a break. We try to celebrate meeting big goals with dance parties in our living room and show our daughter that it is fun to work.
5. **What advice would you give moms who want to leave a corporate career in favor of something untraditional?**
   It may seem impossible to find the time to grow your business, but if you just keep focused on the vision and why you are doing this, it will push you through the hard

times and the late nights/early mornings. For me, I looked at my vision journal daily (even while at work), and I had a vision board in my house. I was constantly filling my mind with what my life would be like someday. For moms struggling with time, think about how much more time you'll have for your kids in the future. It's so worth it. Your kids grow so fast and having no regrets is so important. You won't regret the hard work it will take you to get there. So many possibilities now exist for women who want to make income online or have customers around the world. You just have to take the first step.

## Your Most Important Work

Many possibilities are available to moms today. We live in an amazing time to be a mother, but amidst all the choices women now enjoy, let's not lose sight of what's most important. We must use wisdom to discern our role in each season of our family's life cycle.

You may answer the question of career in a variety of ways as your children grow and change. It's okay to change your mind or even forge your own path to create a hybrid between career and being home with your kids. The sky is the limit.

However, in all these decisions, we must remain true to our most important task as mothers and wives. We inhabit a sacred role in the lives of those we've been entrusted with. We must never take lightly the love, support, encouragement, and blessing our children need from us. If fact, children are wired to connect to their mothers in a way that is unlike any other relationship. Mothers have been given the role of nurturer, and while that role can't be reduced to a one-size-fits-all description, it is still our most holy work.

A woman is also called to be one with her husband, to love him as she loves herself, and to be his cheerleader and helpmate. When you neglect this relationship, the effects will ripple out to affect each member of the home. In contrast, a strong marriage gives children a sense of safety and security. When ongoing strife between partners is present, children sense that all is not well. Sacrificing time with your husband for lesser, temporary things is never a good trade-off.

With that said, I want to tell you about a season of my life when home life had to trump all else in order of importance. My husband and I faced an overwhelming struggle in our marriage, and together we overcame. However, it required an exceptional amount of effort and clarity. While every mom can choose work, it's important to also know when a difficult season calls you to focus your energy at home.

# 9
# Courage to Be Vulnerable

In 2012, I noticed some changes in Josh. He started gaining weight, and his relaxed demeanor grew more tense every day. He started sleeping more and eventually had days where he could not get out of bed. The same things that usually brought him joy, including me and the kids, seemed no longer to do so.

He was diagnosed with clinical depression in the winter of 2012. I was expecting our third baby, our third child in three years. To say this was a difficult period is an understatement. I was working around the clock to support my family with my business, yet we were barely scraping by. I was handling the demands of two small children—both still in diapers—and I was about to pop out a third.

## Courage to Face the Unexpected

Some days, I witnessed my spouse overcome with a grief and sadness that was so uncharacteristic of his personality. It is not an exaggeration to say it paralyzed him. I witnessed him unable to enjoy life. I witnessed him unable to get out of bed and unable to make simple decisions, like what to eat for breakfast. He was unmotivated and not at all the man I had married.

And at first I could not understand. I wanted to fix it. I desperately, utterly, from my core wanted to take the suffering off his shoulders. I felt terrified and alone. I *was* alone. Because I felt ashamed of his condition, I wasn't talking about it with anyone. Eventually the pressure of carrying such a heavy load took its toll. Yet I did not know how to talk about a condition that I myself could barely comprehend. I could not explain how my once happy-go-lucky husband, all of a sudden, was nowhere to be found. He became reclusive and took a leave from work for several months.

When people would ask me how he was doing, I would smile and say, "He's tired from working so hard for us. He's off work right now to get some rest." It was partially true, but not the real reason for his sudden absence. I just couldn't share authentically. That kind of vulnerability seemed more challenging than bearing the burden alone.

I was ashamed of the illness, and I was ashamed of my response. I held hatred for his depression. I so desperately wanted my husband back. I was angry he went away. I wanted him to realize how alone I was and how much I missed him. I wanted my best friend back.

I hated that depression made it exceedingly difficult for my husband to get out of bed for days at a time, unable to enjoy anything. I hated that depression had reduced this positive man, who loved family life so abundantly, to a hollow, depleted man who could barely smile. Along with hating depression, I was angry with God. I was angry with other people, well-meaning people who said things they thought to be kind and helpful but came across as judgmental and insensitive. These "words of encouragement" felt like salt on open wounds and only made me angrier.

I am a take-charge kind of girl. I have faced down challenges in career and family and have worked hard to achieve and pioneer a way of life that works for me and my children. But this was one situation that hard work could not cure. With all my spark and vitality, with my tip-top work ethic, and even with my flair for casting vision, I could not do a single thing to make depression go away quickly. I was terrified. I was not in control. And I was desperate for relief.

Depression is a disease, and like any disease, it can be treated. After months of taking time off work, developing new diet and exercise habits, and meeting regularly with his psychiatrist and taking medication, my old husband came back to us. And I made friends with depression.

## Courage to Get Real

In Canada, we have a campaign every January, started by one of our national cell phone companies, called #BellLetsTalk. This campaign advocates for mental health awareness and care, with donations to mental health initiatives in Canada for every use of the hashtag #BellLetsTalk. Yet, despite the work of this initiative, mental health can still seem like a private matter, a battle to fight alone.

In 2015, three years after our first encounter with depression, I finally decided to talk about it openly on my blog. I talked about the pain of depression and some of the strategies that have helped us thrive. And I would go on to keep talking about it and writing about it, daring to be real and honest. The willingness to be vulnerable changed my life in positive ways.

Truly, the power of authenticity and vulnerability cannot be overstated. I had hidden for a long while behind my anger and fear, afraid of what others might think if they knew about Josh, about our struggles. The silence was stifling. In the dark, my shame and resentment grew, but when I talked about it, bringing it into the light, my load somehow lightened. The repercussions of my decision to share have been nothing short of amazing.

First of all, it started a conversation. Being open about depression online gave others courage to share their stories. The continuing conversation has shown me how many people suffer—and, as I had done, suffer in silence. The stigma and shame remain, despite ongoing efforts to communicate that depression is a common illness and is not a conscious choice or moral weakness.

Second, my risk to share the truth allowed me to be real. It's one thing to go online and post pictures of beautiful rooms, inspiring products, and fun mom hacks. But to feel loved for the real you—the one behind the lens and all the pretty filters—is a whole other exercise. Let me tell you, when depression is active, there ain't no pretty filters. It's raw and it's messy, for both partners in the relationship.

Josh and I cried many times together in sheer desperation. But we also revealed more of ourselves to one other. Through the tears, we shared our good, bad, ugly, and beautiful. I truly feel, as a result, I now know Josh's authentic self. Through our transparency, we came to know each other on a deeper level. The illness knit us together and enabled an intimacy we might have missed if not for the vulnerability it forced in us. And that is beautiful.

Hear me. I am not arguing that it requires a challenging situation like depression to enable us to reveal deep parts of ourselves to our spouses. I am saying that a great gift from our experience with depression, both during and after, is that we wrung ourselves out completely and loved each other back with full force. And while this is our story alone, the principle can be applied to many challenges and setbacks within your home.

## Courage to Give up Control and Change Our Lifestyle

Encountering depression also forced us to look closely at our habits and lifestyle. We had to make changes that would put the mental health of our entire family at the forefront.

I used to fill the social calendar to the brim and essentially expect everyone else to jump on board the busy train. Understanding Josh's need for space and quiet and embracing the freedom to say no to an invitation if he is not feeling up to it, we do not make social plans too far in advance. We like to keep the calendar as flexible as possible, reserving the weekends for rest and quiet. Saying no to birthday party invitations and social engagements at our church is okay now.

We now prioritize time alone, both as individuals and as a couple. A weekly date night is a non-negotiable for us, and we both make time in our schedules for personal retreats. We've learned that time away from intensity is important for good mental health.

Our need to prioritize rest, time alone, time away as a couple, and time away from intensity means our calendar, especially on weekends, looks very different from many of our friends' schedules. It means our use of childcare looks very different from those around us. Our choice to prioritize rest means we say no to a lot of things, and I am sure this choice has disappointed people along the way. We have learned that we cannot control the reactions of others. But we do have power over our choices and how busy our calendar is. And that has made all the difference and allowed our family to thrive.

## Hope in All Situations

While you may never fully understand why you or your spouse is facing an illness or tragedy, you do still have a choice about how you react. Will you allow the circumstance to pull you apart or draw you together? Will you allow your spouse to see your softer emotions, your hurt, frustration, confusion, and all the other inner recesses of your heart? Or will you display instead the more straightforward emotions of anger and fear? Even in the dark and trying times, possibilities abound—maybe even possibilities that lead you to the other side with more joy.

While there was a time when I truly wasn't sure how we would survive depression, today depression no longer defines our marriage. We chose a different ending than the one I feared. We chose to let the illness bind us together. We chose courage and resiliency. We focused on the story we ultimately wanted to write for our family: one of overcoming, resilience, and joy, not resignation and regret.

Depression has come back a few times since the initial phase, and we continue to manage anxiety daily. But I mean it when I say that while it is not an easy process, it is one that we manage with open hearts, trusting in God and our love for one another.

I share this story as I believe it contains overtones of one of the most important virtues we can develop as moms: courage. Courage is being frightened yet facing the challenge anyway. If we want to come closer to our goals, remain true to what matters most, and write the story we desire for our future family, courage is essential. Courage can apply to overwhelming circumstances, like Josh's depression, but it is also necessary for even small changes that push us beyond the script we've been following for years.

## Is It Your Turn to Be Vulnerable?

So I have to wonder, do you have hard parts of your life from which you are tempted to withdraw? Is there some little secret or hardship that you carry alone or with your partner only? Is it time to be brave and face the issue head-on? Is it time to be vulnerable and let safe others know about your struggle and how they can support you?

If you have never seen a professional counselor or therapist, this could be your time. By reading this book, you are daring to dream what might be possible for your life. You are daring to rise above what is true right now and rethink limiting beliefs. Seeing a therapist might be part of this process of calling forth your best self. An impartial guide who can hold space for your pain or your questions could offer amazing support on your journey to felt significance and purpose. I hope my honesty in describing our battle might inspire you to address similar issues that could be holding you back from wellness.

There is no shame in being honest or asking for help. Rather, shame multiplies with secrets and can become a powerful force that weighs you down. So be courageous and face your problems now. Let's talk more about the courage it takes to change.

# 10
# Courage to Change

**"Scared is what you're feeling. Brave is what you're doing."**
–Emma Donoghue, *Room*

You can read every self-help book and invest in every productivity course under the sun, but if you don't have hope to push through difficult times, courage to stand up even though you might fall, and bravery to live your unique and authentic life, nothing will happen—certainly nothing amazing. In short, you will fall short of your potential. All the possibility you hold will just, well, fizzle out.

## Courage to Be Uncomfortable

It takes courage to do what is uncomfortable. In fact, it is knowing how to sit in or withstand discomfort that often makes the difference between success and failure. For example, it was uncomfortable to talk openly about depression's effects on our marriage, yet that type of vulnerability propelled me forward. With that act of courage, I became a little more unstuck, and my blog became a place where I could be myself. Readers knew they were hearing my heart—not just my design tips.

Like it or not, any kind of worthwhile change will require bravery and the willingness to leave the comfortable known for a season of uncomfortable "what if." Keep in mind, possibilities push us to the edge and are all about courage. To live your dream life and design your best future, you must take chances. It takes courage to get to the gym and be hard on your body, knowing it's not going to be easy to achieve the results you seek. It takes courage to stop eating unhealthy food; your comfort foods and cravings might be hard to surrender as you select options that are foreign yet better for your body. It takes courage to finally complete a project that requires hard work and daily sacrifice. It takes courage to be the lone mom in the schoolyard who has chosen to march to the beat of her own drum.

You might be thinking, *Lisa, get real. Working out, dieting, creating, or mothering don't demonstrate courage. Fighting a war is courageous. Standing up for civil rights is courageous. What you've described are just disciplined actions.*

Yes, this list could be described as acts of discipline. But I argue that any hard decision that takes us out of our comfort zone also requires courage—whether it be facing an armed enemy, walking into a public gym, making a career change, or even writing a book.

## Courage and Perseverance

Along with courage, perseverance is required for lasting change. To get through a few very serious bouts of clinical depression, Josh learned to persevere. We both learned that to move forward and make progress, we must show up. We can't hit autopilot or withdraw until it looks safe to come out. We have to face each day with fearless courage—and that requires perseverance, tenacity, and steadfast determination. Whatever term you use to describe it, this concept means you choose to stay present when numbing or running seems preferable.

When my husband was sad and moody, I often wanted to retreat into my own hole and not deal with his irritability. No doubt, that would have been the easier route, but I knew that withdrawal would ultimately serve no one. It would give me a momentary break, perhaps, but it would not advance healing. I had to persevere and engage him, even on dark days. I had to hold on to my dream for our family.

Of course, people with depression need quiet and space sometimes, and that is okay. Taking a walk or doing something physical is really helpful at times for those with clinical depression. However, quiet and space should not be used as a barrier to relationship. Staying in it together was essential for Josh and me. Our commitment to each other required me to show up—even if it might mean rejection.

But experience has shown me that the times I dug deep and forced myself to show up rather than retreat have been the times of greatest progress. And while perseverance isn't easy, it is necessary for creating change. So I ask you, where do you need to display more courage in your life right now? What are your dreams, and how can you hold on to hope during trying circumstances?

## Courage Gets Us out of Ruts

In a recent coaching call, I was speaking with a mom who was overwhelmed. She ran her own business while raising two small kids. From what she had shared in our conversation, it was clear she was time-strapped and overrun by a full schedule. Finding time to relax was difficult. After completing a hectic workday and picking up her children from daycare, her evenings usually consisted of spending two hours at the dinner table with her slow-eating toddler, followed by a bedtime process that required her to sit and literally watch her toddler fall asleep. During this tuck-in routine, she would typically fall asleep herself, sitting up in the rocking chair, only to wake up at midnight with a sink full of dishes still to do and a messy house still to clean. On top of it all, she was usually running late for everything, including our scheduled call.

After I gave her some practical tactics, including sleep training for her toddler and organizational tips for her schedule and home, I asked what made her late for our call. In exasperation, she replied that, on top of everything else, she agreed to make a vegetable tray for a community event and was now going to spend the next thirty minutes chopping vegetables. I went silent for a moment, took a deep breath, and said, "If you don't remember anything else on this call, remember this: next time, just buy the *pre-made* vegetable tray!"

She went silent for a moment, and then I heard laughter on the line. She told me, through her laughter, that she was so used to doing everything herself that it did not even occur to her to buy a pre-made vegetable tray. She was so used to certain patterns of behavior that a change as simple as buying a pre-made vegetable tray never even crossed her radar. She was so lost in her out-of-control life, so given over to the insanity, that it took a third party to point out the obvious. This one woman's story powerfully illustrates two truths:

- The power of an invited outside opinion
- How ruts can keep us stuck

Imagine taking a piece of paper and folding it in half. Now unfold it and try to smooth it out. No matter how much you smooth it, the crease you created is still there. Our brains are the same. We create grooves in our brain when we do something over and over again. And the more we do it, the deeper the groove becomes until, like a deep trench, you can't see out of the rut anymore.

As Charles Duhigg shares in *The Power of Habit*, "Habits, scientists say, emerge because the brain is constantly looking for ways to save effort. This explains why habits are so powerful: They create neurological cravings." The brain is lazy at times and wants to find the easiest path to complete the task at hand. If we dig a deep enough trench, it will feel easy, predictable, and comfortable as we pass through. Our brain will then seek out that well-known pattern again and again.

It's the deep trenches of negative thought patterns and limiting beliefs, such as thinking we're not good enough or thinking others will be turned off if we are less than perfect, that keep us stuck. We believe that comfort is better than risk, so we keep repeating the same routines—even if those routines are robbing our joy or sucking our energy. It's not easy to see past the way things are. And this is why courage is so important. Courage points us upwards, out, and forward. It gives us hope to envision life beyond the trench, to trust that more is possible.

Changing a pattern of behavior takes hard work and requires boldness and daring. It might also require enlisting outside help as you learn new tactics to face your challenges head-on. Outside help might take the form of therapy; healthy self-awareness is required to identify the trench and devise a new plan, and it's hard to see our way clear on our own. A therapist can help you lean into difficult emotions and will hold space for you to share about your particular pain points. It is freeing to talk about what burdens you and to have a safe other encourage you to see your struggles in a new light.

But the fun thing is, if one is willing to do the work, change is possible. You *can* design the life you have been hoping for. But you need to have courage. Courage is what will get you closer to your dreams and ultimately change your life.

I am rooting for your change—so much so I'd like to share with you my top habits that will instantly impact your life (and of course I have a worksheet for you on "High Impact Habits" at www.thepossibilitymom.com/downloads). These habits require the courage to do something different, and that can be scary. You might at first want to dismiss the idea that these little changes could add up to a big impact, but I promise you they will. Be brave. Give these habits a chance.

# 11
# Habits and How to Make Change Stick

Congratulations, dear reader! You have come so far, and I hope you are beginning to see the possibilities that lie before you. I hope you feel change stirring deep within and have caught a vision for a new way to inhabit the role of motherhood, performing that role in a manner unique to you.

To make sure all you've learned sticks and becomes a part of your routine, I would like to share with you my top mom habits, the life hacks I've discovered that truly make a difference when embraced. With each hint, I've given you an action step to start making these changes *now*. Don't go back to the depleted, guilty, stressed-out version of yourself that picked up the book. Time has come for real change. Visit www.thepossibilitymom.com/downloads for my "Habit Tracking Tool" to make this more concrete.

## Visualization

Visualization is a powerful tool used by professional athletes, speakers, and business professionals alike. It essentially involves playing a movie in your mind; you are the star, and you picture yourself in a scenario, performing at your optimal level. Olympic athletes do this, picturing how a run will go during an Olympic competition. A speaker might visualize delivering a talk in front of thousands of people with confidence and charisma. And a business owner might visualize leading an incredible team meeting or a transformative conversation with clients.

In Brendon Burchard's book *High Performance Habits*, he recommends asking your future self where more courage might be needed. He also suggests reflecting on how the best version of yourself might handle a situation.[21] Visualization is a great tool to use to picture the best version of yourself. For example, on my way home from work, an appointment, errands, or a trip, I sit in my driveway and visualize two scenarios:

a) Scenario 1 is how I would like my time at home to go. It is how events will unfold if I am acting as the best version of myself. I literally picture, like a movie, what every interaction should look like: "Hi, guys! I'm so happy to see you! Wow, what beautiful pictures! Wow, you worked hard on that, and I can tell! Oh, I can hear you're disappointed that I wasn't home earlier. What can we do together now that I am home? It's great to see you."
b) Scenario 2 is how I would *not* like my time at home to go, and I often base this visualization off past experience and actual words I have said, which I wish I could take back: "Guys, let Mommy get in the door. Stop pulling on my hair; stop talking all at once. Wow, you guys made a huge mess that I now have to clean up. Gosh, I wish you would wait

21 Brendon Burchard, *High Performance Habits: How Extraordinary People Become That Way* (Carlsbad, CA: Hay House, 2017).

> for Mommy before you make crafts on the dinner table. Okay, let's clean it up. We have a lot to do before dinner and baths. Has everyone done his homework? You know that's what we do before we do any crafts or watch TV."

I let these two movies play in my head, and then I pray for the courage to be the mom in scenario 1. I walk in the door, armed with this boldness, and I do my absolute best to let the first movie be what actually happens.

If I am honest, real life is usually more of an 80/20 split, with 80 percent of my reactions being in line with scenario 1 and 20 percent of my reactions in line with scenario 2. But what I love about this visualization exercise is that it essentially sets a bar for you to measure yourself against. In fact, the act of visualizing can be just as powerful as doing it in real life.

I challenge you, for one week, to do this visualization exercise each time you come back home. I dare you *not* to feel the positive impact of this practice. I don't think you can help but see your "coming home" experience improve. And once you master visualizing your ideal arrival at home, use this same visualization exercise for the other scenarios in life in which you tend to react differently than you would as your best self.

In the moments you might not have time to paint a whole movie of your life in your head, use the following sentence to focus on what truly matters: *What does my future self want?* I like to say this sentence in the heat of the moment or when my will just doesn't seem strong. It keeps me from saying or doing something I will later regret. Often our regrets come from taking the easy dig, the easy shot at those we love the most. Asking myself this question helps me take the high road when I'm frustrated or stressed.

I was introduced to this simple statement by the founder of Fastermind.co, Dane Sanders. I find it to be a phrase you can pull out like a weapon in so many situations. Consider what your future self would want in the following scenarios:

- When you know you shouldn't have another piece of pie, but really want to
- When the options for an evening are to work out or scroll aimlessly in Instagram
- When it is one in the morning and you're on your third hour of YouTube videos
- When you really want to scream at your kids for making a mess
- When you want to nag your spouse for forgetting where he put his wallet—again

**Action Step: Visualize a challenging situation by using the scenario 1 and 2 activity. Continue to visualize this situation until you can live it out as close to scenario 1 as possible. Then choose another area and start over with visualizing how your best self would respond.**

## Weekly Review

Another habit I find helpful is a weekly calendar review. Every Sunday evening, I take a few minutes and look at my week ahead to take stock of what is going on. I note the days that might be super tiring due to appointments and plan to order dinner in that evening. I note the days my husband and I might need to discuss who is driving what car and determine the errands that need to be run.

I find it helpful to involve my spouse in my weekly review and share with him what is going on with me and with the family. It gives us both clarity, cuts down on surprises, and brings efficiency to the running of our household.

You can also extend this habit to monthly or quarterly reviews, but I find the weekly review to be a helpful first step. It's an easy habit to develop and ensures that none of the moving parts of family life get missed.

I've created a beautiful download for you called the "Weekly Calendar Review" to get you started.

**Action step: Schedule fifteen minutes in your calendar to review the week ahead and set yourself up for success.**

## Make Your Morning Count

I am not a morning person by nature. All through university, I would pull all-nighters and function fairly well the next day. So I considered myself a night owl. And then I had children and realized that sleep is a precious, precious commodity that should never be taken for granted! *Ever*! How did I dare complain I was tired when I was a single student? #iflonlyknew

Like many new mothers, I would relish the time when my children were finally asleep for the night. I would curl up in bed, cell phone in my hand, and begin the ritual of the nightly scroll, as in scrolling through my social media feeds in an effort to unwind and relax.

Before I knew it, hours would go by, and I would look at the clock in disbelief. My intention to "just check" something inevitably turned into rabbit trails of YouTube videos, BuzzFeed quizzes, and Nordstrom online shopping bags full of stuff I had seen Instagrammers wearing online. So many times, I would scratch my head and ask how on earth I could have wasted so much time on my phone. Then I would attempt to sleep amidst the blur of images continuing to scroll through my mind.

I considered nights "me time" and looked forward to those hours alone. The thing I never wanted to admit, however, was how much I dreaded the mornings. Being a mom is a full-time job. The demands are on you before you've barely opened your eyes. The requests begin before any caffeine has been consumed, and the cacophony of noise starts when the only noise you want to hear is the sweet sound of snoring. It is *a lot* to wake up to seven children, and it requires courage and discipline to greet the morning well.

I started rethinking my mornings after I stumbled upon Hal Elrod's book *The Miracle Morning*. Elrod shares about the power of waking up early and developing a morning routine composed of activities like sitting in silence, articulating what you're grateful for, visualizing success, writing, reading, and exercise.[22]

I was a mom of four when I discovered this book, and the thought of adding yet another goal to a list of unmet goals was discouraging to me. Waking up before my kids to do all these beautiful-sounding things seemed impossible. Intentional mornings were for people without kids. *I'm a mother*, I told myself. *I'll take the extra minutes of sleep, thank you very much*. But after listening to a few podcasts on the topic (Jeff Sanders' *The 5 AM Miracle* podcast is a great one), I was motivated to try. And the difference it made in my life is pretty amazing.

---

22 Hal Elrod, *The Miracle Morning: The Not-So-Obvious Secret Guaranteed to Transform Your Life (Before 8 AM)* (Miracle Morning Publishing, 2014).

It was quite the adjustment. I went from rolling out of bed to the sounds of my children demanding breakfast to waking up at half past five to the sound of the alarm clock. And at five-thirty, I would enter a clean, quiet kitchen and invest in myself. After a few days of doing this, I became a totally different person. When my family joined me in the kitchen at seven o'clock for breakfast, I wasn't grumpy. I wasn't short-tempered. I was actually a fairly pleasant person to be around.

And my husband was not at all shy to comment on the positive change to my disposition. He totally approved of my new morning schedule. My woe-is-me, chaotic morning was exchanged for a positive, enjoyable, and more manageable start to the day.

So try it. Make your mornings count. Wake up before your kids and seize the day. If the five o'clock hour sounds extreme, aim for fifteen minutes before your children wake up. In fifteen minutes, you can do the following:

- Brush your teeth in quiet (perhaps while thinking about the day ahead)
- Drink coffee in quiet (maybe while naming things you are grateful for)
- Get dressed in quiet (maybe add a fast stretch or a few deep, cleansing breaths)

The above suggestions might sound cheesy to you, or you might be thinking, *What's the point of a few lousy stretches?* But every good habit starts somewhere, and big changes can be accomplished with tiny steps forward.

Finally, my favorite thing Hal Elrod talks about in *The Miracle Morning* is the notion that if you were getting up early to go on a holiday and catch an early flight at an airport, you'd be up and excited. *Shouldn't we be that excited for every day of our lives?* I would like to wake up that way.

**Action Step: Set a goal to get up fifteen minutes earlier than normal to have a morning that counts.**

## Make Your Evenings Sacred

Setting our mornings up for success takes determination the night before. How early we get up is impacted by how late we get to bed. This is something I still struggle with. I love me some quiet, and my time at night, when I can be alone with no one asking anything of me, is intoxicating. So much so that I often squander this time on things that don't ultimately lead to calm and restoration.

We give and give and give of ourselves all day as moms, whether it be working outside of the home or being with our kids inside the home. And sometimes we just want to drink a glass of wine and watch Netflix in peace. And let's face it. Sometimes it is just more attractive to get some stuff done alone at night rather than getting up early the next day.

I recently had a massive wake-up call regarding my health. My dear friend Sarah recommended I see her naturopath, and after having six kids in eight years, constantly fluctuating in weight, and constantly feeling sluggish and tired, I figured I needed all the help I could get.

The naturopath did a scan that revealed my nervous system was working in serious hyper-drive; my adrenal glands were basically waving white flags of defeat. She asked me what in my life might be making my nervous system work so hard, and I just about spat my water out of my mouth, laughing at that question.

What was *not* causing my nervous system to work hard? Between writing this book, raising small kids, supporting my spouse and his mental health challenges, and having some semblance of friendships and investment in my own personal growth and rest, my adrenal glands and nervous system were working very hard—*all the time.* For periods in my life, four hours of sleep has simply been the norm.

She asked me, "What would life look like if you got six or eight hours of sleep? How would you feel?" And the gosh-darn-honest truth is that my productivity might not change (I already get *so much done*), but I would feel *so much better.*

Feeling like a walking zombie is no fun. Feeling like it is an absolute necessity to have caffeine in your hand at all times to stay alert and focused is not normal. And feeling like it is necessary to turn to alcohol to relax isn't always a good thing either. All of this is to say, if we don't take care of ourselves, we can't be any good to our families. And sleep is a necessary part of this process. Our bodies need it.

You might be thinking, *Lisa, you don't need to sell me on the importance of sleep. I crave it every second of the day. But how on earth am I supposed to get more sleep in my already overwhelmed life? If I don't stay up late, the laundry won't get done, the lunches won't get made, and I won't have any alone time. I just cannot go to bed early.*

I get it; you know I do. A mom's life is full of sensory overload. Someone is always crawling on you, pulling on your shirt, throwing a toy at your head, or screaming your name. It can make you feel like retreating into a cone of silence or crawling into a dark hole. So I understand that by nighttime you are ready to do your own thing.

But what if we changed our perspective on evenings and transferred some of that "me time" to the mornings or other times in the day? This shift is important for two reasons:

1. Evening me time can go on forever. You can literally hit the "next" button on Netflix until you cannot keep your eyes open, and this will inevitably take a toll. In our bodies, we pay a price for sleepless nights that only coffee can help—and a caffeine fix is only temporary.
2. Me time for a mom should not be limited to the hours after nine at night. A mom must make self-care a priority in her schedule. Time for you *must be prioritized* the same way you would prioritize going to a school play or grocery shopping.

**Yes, motherhood requires sacrifice, but not the complete sacrifice of physical and mental health.**

This leads me to what I believe is the biggest problem in motherhood today: the myth that being a good mom means you sacrifice everything for your kids. This is *not* God's design for motherhood. Yes, motherhood requires sacrifice, but not the complete sacrifice of physical and mental health.

So start with your sleep. Prioritize your well-being in this one area and see the results. I would encourage all moms to make evening sacred and part of the me-time routine. A healthy evening routine might be watching a thirty- or sixty-minute show at least an hour before bed, relaxing in the bath, reading a book, and then going to bed by ten if a half-past-five wake-up time sounds good to you. I am not a sleep health expert, but I am an expert in what a mom needs to thrive, and she needs time to herself that doesn't come at the expense of her health.

**Action Step: Design an intentional, restorative evening routine and keep it sacred.**

## Reclaim Me Time

I touched on this concept while speaking of sleep. "Me time" is a really important topic, so I want to give you a few more ideas for how to expand your self-care beyond sleep. Here are a few ways you can carve out time for yourself regularly.

## Schedule Self-Care Like a Recurring Appointment

This tip is as simple as the subtitle suggests. Create a block of time in your calendar, click the button that makes it a recurring appointment, and honor this block of time in the same way you would honor a coffee date with a friend, a yearly checkup, or any other commitment that might require you to leave the kids at home.

Think of me time as regular maintenance on your car; if you don't proactively take care of yourself, you will break down, likely at an inopportune time. You cannot take care of your family if you run out of gas or have engine trouble. Time to relax and refresh is like filling up your tank. Don't skip it. You will eventually notice weariness, frustration, and increased sensitivity if you have not properly cared for yourself. In this way, think of self-care as a gift to those around you. Trust me, you will be more pleasant to be around if you make me time a priority.

## Make It Simple

Self-care does not need to be elaborate or epic by any means. It may mean you take a nap, have a quiet cup of coffee alone, or splurge on a manicure. I do, however, suggest being strategic with the time. In my current season of life, I have brief time slots where I can truly be alone and relax. But, boy, do I ever make the most of those times! Just keep your options simple and manageable and don't compare your self-care to what other people are doing.

## Stop Comparing Your Season of Life to Someone Else's

As I have shared before, comparison is the thief of joy. And what does this have to do with self-care? I believe self-care starts in our heads. We must bravely dig new trenches in our brain and then be happy in them. Our opportunities to relax will be enhanced if we allow contentment to fill us with gratitude.

If you can only manage a thirty-minute manicure, don't dwell on your neighbor who just took a weeklong trip to California wine country. If a nap sounds heavenly, don't compare your rest time to your sister's weekly spa day.

**Action Step: Find alternate times in your day—beyond evening hours—to get the me time you need. Take out your calendar and schedule self-care. Make it a priority.**

And this point brings us to a discussion about social media and the tiny computer we carry with us every moment of the day.

## Interview with Jenn Pike, Nutrition and Lifestyle Expert

1. **Jenn, I'm so excited to talk to you about self-care.[23] As a holistic nutrition and lifestyle expert, personal trainer, and creator of The Simplicity Project and The Hormone Project, you must have wisdom to share. And, as you know, self-care is challenging for moms, often getting pushed to the bottom of the priority list. What would you say to encourage a mom who is always putting her self-care and general health last?**

   Oftentimes we make the quest for health more complicated than it needs to be. Instead of thinking you need forty-five to sixty minutes, begin to look for the spare moments in your day. Can you place water next to your bed at night and be sure to drink five hundred milliliters when you wake? Can you keep your supplements next to your toothbrush so you don't forget to support your body? Can you talk to your friend, coworker, or client on the phone while you walk outside, instead of sitting at your desk?

   As for your nutrition, when you make a smoothie, can you double or triple that batch and put the extra in the fridge for later? Could you stock healthy protein bars, trail mix, and other snack options in a special drawer, container, or cupboard so that when you're on the run, you have something within reach that will support you? Can you add veggies to each meal and snack? Veggies,

23 Find Jenn at www.jennpike.com.

especially greens and cruciferous varieties, are so important for healthy hormones, ladies!

2. **Developing healthy habits can seem like an overwhelming task or another item to add to a list of already overwhelming demands. What is one simple thing a mom can do to contribute to a healthier lifestyle?**
   Adopt the tips I just shared and then assign yourself and your own goals the same level of importance you grant to your children and spouse. Book out a couple of soul appointments each week: take a bath with essential oils, drink a warm elixir each morning, and go to bed earlier instead of scrolling on social media or making your home look spotless. Start small, but just start.
3. **You are a mom of two who manages an online business and many in-person events and fitness classes. What is your greatest hack, or best habit, to ensure you keep health a priority?**
   I choose health above and beyond everything else. When I wake up, my exercise, hydration, supplements, and morning elixir come before anything else. I don't answer any emails or work until I have had that time for myself to focus and get grounded. No matter how tired I am or how full my schedule is, I do something for me. Some days it's a walk with the dog, some days the gym or yoga; other days, I sit in the car longer in the driveway when I get home just to take a few extra breaths. I don't really watch TV and instead get to bed no later than ten o'clock each night. Sleep and never comprising on my

food choices has been my secret weapon, both inside and out. We also discuss our health goals as a family often, to ensure we all feel supported on our individual journeys.

## Change Your Relationship with Your Phone

As I have mentioned, I am really good at scrolling on social media apps for infinite periods of time. I could win a gold medal at the scrolling Olympics. And don't even get me started about my Netflix habits. I can have the discipline it takes to write a book or balance kids and business, but ask me to resist watching one more episode when it starts on auto-play? I am done for.

But let me be clear. The things we do to relax or be entertained, like scrolling on social media or watching videos online, are not inherently bad things. Moms *need* to relax. However, as I described earlier, when the tools we use to relax negatively impact our health or our relationships, we need to evaluate their importance.

During one season, I was so frustrated by my own obsessive relationship with social media that I went on a total social media and email fast for thirty days. I took all the apps off my phone. I put a vacation responder on my email. My phone became what phones were like when I first got a cell phone—literally just a phone.

For the first few days, I could not kick the habit of reaching for my phone as soon as I had the opportunity to sit down. As soon as one moment of boredom came, like while in line at a grocery store or waiting to pick up my kids in the car outside school, I would reach for my phone out of habit.

I removed social apps from my phone, yet I kept opening my phone, looking for the Instagram button. I would actually tap the blank screen where it used to be. When I would open my phone and realize there was nothing on it to offer distraction, I became restless and unsettled. Kicking the habit of constantly engaging my mind and my thumbs was a really hard shift.

But then, toward the end of that first week, I got used to my new normal. I left my phone in my purse, rather than having it on my body at all times. I read books with my kids without being distracted. I took walks without being distracted. I basically did normal things in life, which I used to do before I had a smartphone, without interruption, one thing at a time. What a novel concept!

I am a high achiever. In fact, my second Strength Finder strength is "Achiever." I have a ton of stamina and can get a lot of things done in a day. Interestingly, my biggest takeaway from my social media fast was that by doing less I achieved more. And the things to which I gave my attention got more of me.

Here are my top observations from my walk in the internet desert. These takeaways explain why everyone should take a technology fast to examine your relationship with your phone.

## You Gain Clarity on How to Spend Your Time

Whenever my husband nagged me about how much time I spent on my phone, I would roll my eyes, thinking, *Oh, dear husband, how little you know about running a business. Don't you understand I need to be connected at all times to respond to comments, answer queries, and remain relevant to my customers and growing tribe?*

Since I also did a work sabbatical at the same time as my social media fast and did not want to fall off the face of the internet universe completely, I did pre-program a few posts here and there. And I had my sister monitor my email a few hours a week and continue to respond to leads and press requests.

And what happened? Everything continued to operate. I still got comments on things. I still booked design consultations. I still got press requests. And while I did not personally respond to everything, everything important got handled.

The lack of noise and the relief from being constantly interrupted helped me see where my gifts could be maximized and where my talents could make the most impact—with both my family and my business. Without the smartphone distraction, I had time for self-reflection.

## You Might Become a Better Friend

This might sound a little like grade-six schoolyard, but hear me out. I love social media, and I love some of the friendships I have made on my various platforms. But the absence of social media made me miss certain people. And guess what? Instead of confining our interaction to cyberspace, I picked up the phone and actually called those friends. And they called me. It did remind me of grade six and what friendship was like back when you actually spoke on the phone. Revisiting that simpler time was awesome.

While social media is an amazing tool for connecting people—and I absolutely see its value, 100 percent—its absence made me a more intentional friend, and that was an unexpected bonus.

## You Get More Done by Doing Less

This takeaway is revolutionary: be less busy and you'll actually get more done. I had no idea the grip social media had on my life. I kid you not, there was a time when I was probably engaging in non-intentional (meaning just random scrolling, tweeting, liking, and hearting) social media consumption for upwards of six hours a day. Yup, you read that right. This six hours was not all at once, of course. It was spread out: in line at Target, waiting for my order at a restaurant, while my kids played at the park. But it was also persistent and demanding. As soon as I got out of an appointment, the moment I opened my eyes in the morning, and the last thing before going to sleep, I checked my phone. It's easy to think those little moments don't add up to much, right? I mean, what's fifteen minutes? But string together those fifteen-minute increments all day long and you get six hours. Imagine what you could do with six hours a day!

No longer constantly checking my feed, my mind was quiet. I was able to think about *one thing at a time*. And let me tell you, that kind of focus bore a lot of fruit. I wrote. I schemed. I planned. I dreamed. I prayed. And in the void social media left behind, some serious stuff came to the surface—issues I am grateful I addressed.

## You Might Be Nicer

My obsession with my phone made me incredibly distracted *all the time*, and my family suffered. Because my mind was on three other things at all times, I was short with the people I love most. I was not mentally present for my family nor focused on their good. Sadly, it was my family who absorbed the most damage when I was living life distracted. At the rate I was going, I was destined for the behavior described in a very convicting NPR article from 2014: "For the Children's Sake, Put Down That Smartphone."[24] I encourage you to find this article online and read it for yourself.

---

24 http://www.npr.org/sections/health-shots/2014/04/21/304196338/for-the-childrens-sake-put-down-that-smartphone

During my fast, without constantly feeling pulled in other areas, I was more present and more grounded. Everyone benefited.

## You Will Not Compare Yourself to Strangers

An observation I found when I started engaging in social media again was that I went right back into comparing myself to *total strangers*—and feeling envy for the fortune and accomplishments of people I did not know. No good comes from envy, and I was surprised at how quickly the feeling came over me. Social media, it seems, actually *invites* discontent into our lives. Remember when we discussed swimming in our own lane? When you are "following" another's life, your own possibilities seem to shrink and become less exciting in light of theirs. Are we robbing ourselves of peace and contentment by comparing ourselves to other women?

I write all this because I never thought I could live without social media. Yet I did, and I survived. I think you could too. I don't mean to sound judgmental. I am merely making personal observations, and I am in no way demanding that you cut social media out completely or take as long of a break as I did. What I am asking is for you to seriously examine the hold it has on your life. Ask yourself, *How much time am I spending living life through my phone?* Consider using an app like Moment, which can help you limit your time on certain apps.

Maybe you see the value of doing a social media fast, but now is not the right time. Here are three steps you can still take to reevaluate the role of social media in your life:

1. Remove social media apps on your phone and only use them on your computer.

2. Set time slots for social media just as you would block off time for a gym class. For example, only check at nine o'clock in the morning, noon, and eight at night, for fifteen minutes each.
3. Ask your spouse, family, or close friends how they feel about the way you use your phone. (Brace yourself for the feedback!)

**Action step: Set scheduled times to check social media, and limit your use to those times.**

## Why Willpower Isn't Enough

In this section, I've shared my favorite mom habits, which I've gathered by observing other high-impact moms and examining my own life. But you might be thinking, *Lisa, I have tried all kinds of strategies to break bad habits before, and none of it has worked. How will this time be any different?* Well, stay with me because I am about to go all behavioral science on you, and this brief science lesson is well worth your time.

I recently came across the work of Jim Fortin, an expert in neurolinguistics and behavioral science. In his work, he argues that the reason people fail at changing their habits is because they rely too much on willpower, which is, he explains, a finite resource. Your will can be severely impacted by how tired you are, the endorphins in your body, your ability to think clearly, and loads of other reasons. So he suggests that instead of relying on willpower, we should reprogram our brains to make new habits stick for good.

To reprogram our brains, we need to understand how our brains make decisions and how habits are formed. Habits are highly influenced by two areas of our brain:

**Prefrontal Cortex:** responsible for decision making, personality expression, and complex behavior; thoughts about our habits live here.

**Reptilian Brain:** responsible for keeping us safe and ensuring we are protected; "fight or flight" impulses come from here.

Let's suppose we are trying to engage in a new habit, like waking up early, for example. The prefrontal cortex is the part of our brain that says "Get out of bed." It will fight with our reptilian brain, which essentially tells us to push the snooze button one more time. This "habit battle," as Fortin calls it, can go on and on, back and forth, between getting out of bed or hitting the snooze button. More often than not, the reptilian brain will win. Remember, it is trying to protect us, and ten extra minutes of sleep sure seems like a benefit. And then the prefrontal cortex beats us up with thoughts like, *See, you can't do it; it's not worth it; you'll never break this habit.*

Instead, Fortin suggests you reprogram your brain toward the habit you want to achieve. Here's where it gets really interesting. The reptilian part of your brain wants you to survive, but it's incapable of judging whether the things that currently help you "survive" are good or bad for you. It simply responds to what it knows based on past experiences. It's the prefrontal cortex that attaches meaning, or judgment, to these habits.

Habits are simply functions of the reptilian brain—impulses perceived to keep us comfortable and safe—regardless of whether the habits are actually beneficial. It is why smokers keep on smoking and why it is so difficult to cut sugar from our diets. This survival part of our brain just wants things to stay pleasant and secure. Thus, you can thank your reptilian brain for all your failed diets, extra drinks, and online shopping binges.

**"I cannot want what I am not thinking about."**

–Jim Fortin

So how do we finally break our bad habits and form new ones? How do we tell our reptilian brain, our "habit voice" as Fortin calls it, to be quiet? You dismiss the habit voice. You literally tell your habit voice that the extra slice of pizza or ten minutes of additional sleep does not exist. You shut down those thoughts and move your attention elsewhere. As Fortin explains, you cannot want what you are not thinking about.

I adopted this mental exercise recently in breaking the habit of checking my phone as soon as I got out of bed. My past habit was to reach immediately for my phone to see what likes, comments, shares, and messages I had gotten overnight. This habit not only stalled the start to my day for a good ten to fifteen minutes, but it was also hindering healthier waking habits, like prayer and sitting in quiet before my children get up. Though I know prayer and quiet are objectively a more positive way to start my day, getting affirmation in the form of hearts and likes was fuel for my reptilian brain. Trust me when I say I did not want to give up the instant gratification that came with this habit.

So for a few days, instead of arguing with the voice in my head that said, *Go on; check who likes you this morning*, I told myself,

*I do not have access to my phone for the first thirty minutes after waking*. And then I would move on to brushing my teeth, drinking water, and making coffee. After a few days of dismissing this voice, it became more and more natural to get up and get going. And I am happy to report that the need to check social media first thing each day has been replaced with healthier morning habits.

**Action step: Choose one bad habit you would like to break. What do you need to say to your "habit voice"?**

# 12
# Permission to Fail

**"What if you fall? Oh, but my darling, what if you fly?"**
–Erik Hanson

No one goes into a new venture hoping she will fail. No one launches a product assuming no one will buy it. No one gives a presentation expecting the slides not to work. Instead, hope springs eternal, and most of us resist failure, even in the face of great odds. This intrinsic resistance to failure is the reason so many get stuck, remain stuck, and don't progress toward the things they really want. Let me give you an example from my own life: finishing this book.

Every year I make the trip from Toronto to Nashville for a mastermind meetup with some women I have been doing life and business with for the last three years. On one trip, my friend Susie suggested we meet with her friend Karen, a book editor, to discuss the impact a book could have on our platforms. At the time, I was about seven months' pregnant with my sixth baby. I knew it was going to be an exhausting trip for me physically, so part of me decided that excusing myself to take a nap—as I had no interest in writing a book—would be the most logical thing to do. A book, I told myself, was the kind of thing one did after gaining a large audience. My following was small, so why should I bother with a meeting about publishing?

But of course I went and ended up enjoying an incredible Southern meal—barbecued ribs, creamy coleslaw, baked beans, and delicious cornbread—in Karen's beautifully decorated home. The conversation was as rich and delicious as the food. We went around the table, and Karen invited us to share a bit about our platforms. She asked strategic questions and pushed us to think about the words in our messaging. It was an incredibly valuable exercise, and overall I experienced a generous evening with a gracious host. However, the entire time, I felt myself putting up protective walls.

In a follow-up phone call, once I was home in Toronto, Karen encouraged me to write a book to help today's modern mom. She painted the picture of what it could do for me personally, but more important, she described what it could offer all the moms who desperately need guidance navigating the pressures of modern motherhood. She spoke of her own daughters and the things she observed them going through. "I think the time is now," she told me.

A book was nowhere in my plans. I did not feel equipped, worthy, qualified, or ready to write a book. But I moved forward, submitted a book proposal to Karen, and on November 9, 2016, about six weeks before giving birth to my sixth baby, I got the paperwork from the publisher that my book proposal had been accepted. It was time to write a manuscript that would be turned into an actual, legitimate, sold-all-over-the-world book.

And while I was excited on the outside (of course, I bought a pair of shoes to celebrate), I was terrified on the inside: terrified to share vulnerable things people could criticize me for; terrified to submit a manuscript to an editor who would tell me I was a horrible writer; terrified to be honest and share my life. What if people didn't like me? What if no one liked my book?

Let me just say it: I was terrified to fail.

My fear pushed me to put off writing and finishing this book. I set an initial deadline of April 30, 2017, and I let that deadline come and go. I set another deadline of October 31, 2017, and I let that deadline pass too. I let two additional deadlines come and go as well, and in the midst of it all we sold our house, moved, and got pregnant with baby number seven.

I was stuck. Massively stuck. I knew I had it in me to write this book, but I had to figure out how to get unstuck. How do you get unstuck?

## Let Go of Perfection

A few times already, I have written about the impact of perfectionism in various aspects of life, but I feel it requires mentioning here as well. The need to be flawless, to protect myself with the armor of perfection, is something I have struggled with as far back as I can remember. I recently heard this quote by James Wedmore, and it nearly brought me to my knees: "Perfectionism is your strategy to avoid being judged."

BAM.

The crux of the challenge with perfectionism—its nasty underbelly, if you will—is that it makes the thing we are pursuing more about ourselves and less about the people we are doing it for. We are working for our image, not for others' good.

For so many years, I used perfection as a shield. If I could be great at each pursuit, then perhaps people wouldn't see the real me. If I could do things better than anyone else, then perhaps the parts of myself that I didn't like would go unnoticed. Subconsciously, I thought, *If I am perfect, failure and criticism are not an option,* and this is far more comfortable for me than being vulnerable.

The problem with this line of thinking? Being perfect is *exhausting.* It is *tiring.* It is *inauthentic*. And it keeps true happiness and fulfillment at arm's length. It keeps us from ever reaching the finish line, of ever doing enough. Perfection is an unattainable goal and the saboteur of contentment.

**"Perfectionism is your strategy to avoid being judged."**

—James Wedmore

It's important to note that it is easy to confuse perfectionism with pursuing excellence. Excellence is achievable, and doing our best is a good goal. In contrast, perfection is not achievable; it's a moving target. To the perfectionist, something always could be done better; something is always deemed not good enough. And this paralyzing obsession with getting it just right is a reason many books remain only ideas and many businesses remain only visions.

We've got to stop pursuing the impossible and allow ourselves to just be. After all, the result of "done" and "good enough" could be truly incredible. As Rachel Hollis so boldly puts it in *Girl,*

*Wash Your Face*, "Decide that you care more about creating your magic and pushing it out into the world than you do about how it will be received."[25]

> **"Decide that you care more about creating your magic and pushing it out into the world than you do about how it will be received."**

—Rachel Hollis

## Surround Yourself with People Who Believe in You

In the many times in my life when I've felt stuck, words from people who believed in me (more than I did myself) helped me get moving. Find these relentlessly encouraging people and then hold on to them, hard. For a long time, my tendency toward perfection meant that vulnerability in friendships was very difficult. But over time (and thanks to loads of therapy), I learned to tear down my walls and journey through life in a more authentic, vulnerable way. I now have friendships with women who really know how to love, support, and kick me in the pants in the best way.

Finding your people can be difficult, but it can be magic when the right alignment occurs. The easiest place to start is to look for common interests, whether it be a similar faith, stage in life, or goals. And then start investing in people, openly and freely, without expecting anything in return. I promise the right people will eventually show up in your life.

25 Rachel Hollis, *Girl, Wash Your Face: Stop Believing the Lies about Who You Are So You Can Become Who You Were Meant to Be* (Nashville: Thomas Nelson, 2018).

## The Power of a Mastermind Group

I have been in a mastermind group with several beautiful women for the last three years. Every Monday, we gather electronically to share our wins, express our challenges, and seek advice. I cannot say enough about how powerful it is to have this kind of regular support and accountability. This group has pointed out errors in my thinking I could not see; the members have built me up when I needed support and encouragement and have used their gifts to help me grow in all kinds of ways. Their feedback has been an invaluable part of my journey and my success as an entrepreneur.

I also have dear friends who I informally mastermind with, over lunch, over cocktails, over walks with our babies in strollers, or over manicure-pedicures. These less-formal mastermind relationships are equally helpful and inspiring.

Sometimes we cannot see the forest for the trees, and it really does take the encouragement and perspective of people who believe in us—even more than we believe in ourselves—to make clear the path to progress and show us how to get unstuck.

## Give Yourself Permission to Fail

> **"It's not how far you fall, but how high you bounce that counts."**

—Zig Ziglar

What if, as we begin a new challenge, we extended grace and encouragement to ourselves as we fall? What if we flipped failure completely on its head? What if, as Zig Ziglar recommends, we focused on how well we bounce back rather than obsessing over the mistake?

Instead of fearing failure, let's make friends with it. Let's prepare ourselves with tools to navigate failure when it does happen. Then it could no longer keep us from moving forward. Here are some of the tools and strategies I've used to get more comfortable with failure:

1. I remind myself I am not perfect. Removing the pressure to get everything right is freeing. I remind myself *all the time* that while I am talented in some areas, I am not perfect—nor do I have to be.
2. I ask, "What can failure teach me?" As an online business owner, I have invested in Facebook ads and tried sales funnels, and I have watched them flop. Like, big-time flop. But what I have learned from these experiences has been invaluable. You cannot evaluate and change that which you do not attempt. Trying and failing gives you something to measure and improve upon. Doing nothing will keep you in the exact same spot.
3. I remember that failure is character building. I don't believe we are put on this earth to be comfortable all the time. Being uncomfortable is a necessary part of life and is important for growth.
4. I accept that experiencing failure allows me to help others deal with failure. The more I fail, the more experience I have to draw from when I coach my clients to deal with failure or help my children when they don't get everything they want.

## What Is on the Other Side of Stuck?

For a myriad of legitimate reasons, a goal may not be accomplished: personal illness, death in the family, the loss of a job, etc. And we absolutely need to respond appropriately and be where we need to be when these things happen. But I argue that in spite of challenges and obstacles, we can still make progress on our goals. Our progress may not be perfect, but an imperfect start gets you a heck of a lot further down the path than a perfect holding state.

**"Everything you want is on the other side of fear."**

—Jack Canfield

What would it look like, even in the most challenging and chaotic times, if you reserved just fifteen minutes a day to invest in the dream you have in your heart? What would become possible if one evening a week you dedicated time to a passion project? What would your life look like if you got out of your own way, released the fear of failure and the fear of being judged, and moved forward anyway? Motivational speaker and *Chicken Soup for the Soul* author Jack Canfield cautions against the impulse to give up or check out: "Everything you want is on the other side of fear."

As we near the end of our time together, I want to offer you encouragement on getting unstuck. This is your life. Only you get to live it. And you are the most important participant in how it all plays out. As Rachel Hollis shares in her book *Girl, Wash Your Face,* "Your dream is worth fighting for, and while you're not in control of what life throws at you, you are in control of the fight

. . . . You, and only you, are ultimately responsible for who you become and how happy you are."

I hope these practical strategies for getting unstuck have resonated with you. I used them to finally get this book out of my head, off my computer, and into your hands. I trust these tips will push you further along in your journey toward your most ideal life.

Speaking of push, I have one more story for you.

# 13
# It's Time to Push

When you have been pregnant and given birth seven times, some interesting patterns and comparisons emerge. Seven times I've had *that* feeling, bought an at-home pregnancy kit, and with bated breath waited for little lines to appear. Seven times I have shared the news with my husband, sometimes with grand ceremony (the first ones!) and other times so casually (oh, by the way, I took a pregnancy test and it was positive). Sometimes the timing has made sense to me; other times it's made me question God's understanding of how many hours are in a day.

Seven times I have switched over my wardrobe and figured out how to dress my bump without spending a fortune. Seven times I have taken daily supplements and gone to the doctor for regular checkups. Seven times I have endured the ups and downs—nausea, gas, uncontrollable crying, back pain, hip pain, headaches, exhaustion, stretch marks—that come with growing a human being inside you.

I have given birth seven times, all fairly straightforward deliveries, all in hospital, and all with the wonderful benefits of an epidural. As a result, I have come to actually enjoy and, might I dare to say, look forward to giving birth. My husband and I have a labor routine at this point; we know which bags to bring and which essentials must come (an extra-long cell phone charger and essential oil rollers are a must). Our routine also includes a stop at the same McDonald's each time to pick up coffee and ice cream. (Although I think we have abandoned that last habit. Once, my labor was advanced, but I was so nostalgic to keep up the tradition I insisted we pull into the McDonald's parking lot. I regretted my decision immediately, certain I was going to have the baby in the car while waiting for my husband to get our order. This made for an entertaining ride to the hospital, with my husband furtively praying for every green light!)

Sometimes labor has been so quick for me that I barely realized it happened. A few times I have had to be on antibiotics before giving birth, and they actually slowed down my labor and made me try to sleep for four hours. Sometimes the pain before my epidural has been excruciating, and other times it felt like no big deal.

But in seven pregnancies and births, the one thing that remains the same is the excitement I have felt when the doctor says it's time to push. It's always the same: I am lying there, my bottom half numb, my husband usually passed out in a chair beside me. It's usually the middle of the night (for some reason, Canning children always come in the wee hours of the morning), and thus the lights are usually dim. But then, in a sudden flurry of excitement, the lights go on, a parade of people flood into the room, and the peaceful, quiet atmosphere is replaced with one of anticipation and expectation.

The doctor assumes his position at my feet, with teams of people milling around. My husband is roused from his uncomfortable hospital-chair slumber, and the doctor tells me, "It's time to push!"

And after a few minutes, the most exhilarating, miraculous thing happens. The culmination of forty weeks of care, sacrifice, nurturance, pain, expectation, longing, and desire comes out of me and into the world. Someone I have been hoping for, waiting for, and quietly preparing for makes his incredible entrance, and my world is forever changed.

## It's Time for You to Push

Giving birth to anything new—whether birthing a biological child, adding a child by adoption, starting a new business, leaving a comfortable job, quitting a bad habit, or finally saying no to people who take advantage of you—is full of uncertainty. We don't have a clear picture of what our life will look like on the other side. But when we push through the pain and uncertainty, the fear of failure and risk of rejection, incredible things can happen.

It's time for you to push.

Perhaps life got busy and you weren't able to download the worksheets available with this book. Perhaps you started the work but then got discouraged and stopped filling out the worksheets. Perhaps you skimmed the pages and have landed here. Whatever your level of engagement with the content in this book, it is in your hands at this very moment. And it might just be that it is time for you to push past the plateau, past the doubt or reluctance.

It's time. Even if you have found it difficult to get started or be consistent, here are three simple things you can do right now to push forward (I've also got a worksheet for you called "The Final Push" at www.thepossibilitymom.com/downloads):

1. Choose one concept in this book to implement over the next two weeks. Go and share your choice in the Facebook Group The Possibility Mom Success Circle.
2. Schedule a one-hour appointment with yourself in the next seven days to download and work on the worksheets. Put it in your calendar right now.
3. Take a moment to identify an area of your life you wish were different. What is one step you can take to make a difference in this particular area?

You can do it. You can dream and then design a life that will shock and surprise you. You can chart your own course. You can measure success by your own standards, and you can be happy.

But it's up to you to push. That's the first step to bringing forth a new life. And no one can do it for you. You can hire a team of doulas, go to the most advanced birthing center, and be in a world-renowned hospital with the best obstetric team, but at the end of the day, you alone can give birth to your dream, your possibility. Only you can give birth to your ideal life. And I cannot wait to see what you do with it.

To get started living your most ideal life, and pursue your dreams while being a great mom at the same time,

**go visit www.thepossibilitymom.com**

# Acknowledgments

To my Lord and Savior, who put in my heart these crazy passions and has likely had a good chuckle watching me figure out how to use them here on earth, thank You. Thank You for the breath in my lungs and for showing me that Your plans are always better than my own.

To my children, John, Evelyn, Leo, Rose, Joseph, James, and Phoebe, it is such a gift to be your mother. You all are unique, and watching the way you love each other and love me inspires me every day. You have so much love to give. Thank you for always making room for more.

To my mom and dad, who were the first people to show me what is possible in life, thank you for every single minute you have sacrificed and for all you continue to do to help my family thrive. Your love is extravagant.

To Ken and Sue, thank you for raising the man who would become my husband and for showing me what is possible when love makes room.

To my sister Jocelyn, your support in my life and my business is truly invaluable. It's a special situation we have where we can have meetings with a hundred children running around us and yet be so productive. You make motherhood look so graceful and effortless. Thank you for sharing your gifts with me.

To Sarah, Emily, Jackie, Mona, Christy, and Susie, while I wish distance did not separate us physically, I think the friendships we have formed are pretty special. You all know me and see me; with you, I feel like I belong. Your friendship is a gift.

To Princess, because of you, we thrive at home. We love, appreciate, see, and treasure all the ways you love our family. Thank you.

To the women who have taken my programs and invested in my coaching, who have trusted me with their stories and their hearts, thank you. I've struggled with confidence in this area. I never thought I could make a career out of helping moms thrive, and to do this work is such a gift. I am grateful for every single one of you.

To Karen Anderson, who believed in me more than I believed in myself, thank you for encouraging me to write; to Jennifer Hanchey, bless you for not hating the first drafts of my manuscript; to the entire team at Morgan James, thank you for showing me what is possible in the book publishing world.

And finally, to my husband, Josh. Doing life with you is fun, surprising, and entertaining, but most of all it is *fulfilling.* There's not much to say that you don't already know, but hear this loud and clear: I love our life. This book is the result of our shared desire to embrace possibility, to live life fully, and to discover the unique call God has for our family. And it is an honor and pleasure to walk that walk every day. You are courageous. You are a visionary. You are honest. You are trustworthy. You are so gosh darn good-looking. Waking up next to you every day still makes me giddy. You have made, and continue to make, so many things possible by your love, and for that I am incredibly grateful.

# About the Author

Lisa Canning is a parenting, interior design, and lifestyle expert who helps moms design their lives around what matters most. Lisa's passion for moms to overcome perpetual overwhelm and constant mom-guilt, in favor of a life that is fulfilling and abundant, is apparent in everything she does.

Lisa has become a recognizable face in the interior design and entertainment industry, as the designer on HGTV's *Marriage Under Construction*, working on the design team of *The Property Brothers*, and hosting regular live lifestyle segments on shows like *The Marilyn Denis Show*. For ten years, Lisa transformed the lives of hundreds of families by creating beautiful spaces at home.

At the same time as growing her design business, Lisa grew her family to seven children, all within nine years. As a result,

Lisa has developed a unique approach to time management and productivity, which she shares in her online courses and coaching programs. As an in-demand motivational speaker, podcaster and YouTuber, Lisa offers hope and equips moms with practical tools on how to pursue their dreams and be great moms at the same time.

Learn more about how to pursue your dreams and be a great mom at the same time at www.lisacanning.ca

CPSIA information can be obtained
at www.ICGtesting.com
Printed in the USA
BVHW071128100619
550597BV00002B/3/P

9 781642 792645